BASIC
ROPE
SKILLS
FOR
CLIMBERS

BASIC ROPE SKILLS FOR CLIMBERS

NIGEL SHEPHERD

F

FRANCES LINCOLN LIMITED

PUBLISHERS

Frances Lincoln Limited
4 Torriano Mews
Torriano Avenue
London NW5 2RZ
www.franceslincoln.com

Published in Great Britain in 2009
and the USA in 2010 by Frances Lincoln Limited

A catalogue record for this book is available
from the British Library.

ISBN 978-0-7112-2866-5

Printed in China

Note

All styles of climbing involve an element of risk, and if in
doubt, a professional climbing instructor should be
consulted before using any of the techniques described in
this book. The author and publisher specifically disclaim any
responsibility for any liability, loss or risk (personal, financial
or otherwise) that may be claimed as a consequence –
directly or indirectly – of the use and/or application of any
of the contents of this publication.

CONTENTS

INTRODUCTION

This book is a distillation of techniques previously published in *The Complete Guide to Rope Techniques* (Frances Lincoln, 2007).

It offers advice to those just starting out climbing who are making their first trips to an indoor venue or outside. It is very much a 'self-help' guide to the basics you'll need to get started safely. There are helpful suggestions for those who wish to go it alone and also for those climbers with some experience who might want to introduce their friends or their family to this worthy sport.

Many people begin climbing by attending short one-day or week-long climbing courses with professional instructors and this is perhaps the most sensible way forward. Not only will the experience be considerably safer but it will also be more rewarding in that it can be tailored to suit individual needs.

Much can be learnt in a week and much can be forgotten a week later! That's where these pages will come in handy and serve as a useful reference to jog your memory back into climbing mode.

If you are already an experienced climber wishing to help others experience rock climbing, in particular those climbers who want to get their kids into climbing, use the book as a basic syllabus for getting them started. There's more than enough learning here to get you off on the right footing.

Above all use the book sensibly – it's not a substitute for safe practice or that most valuable of learning medium – experience. Have fun, have adventures by all means, but please, remain safe.

I would like to express my gratitude to the following people and organisations for permission to use photographs: Fraser Ball for allowing me to use pictures of his daughter Josie climbing; the Manchester Climbing Centre and the Castle Climbing Centre London for permission to use the centre for technical images; Wild Country and Lyon Equipment for providing me with images to accompany some of the equipment descriptions; Tim Downes from Ropes and Ladders, Llanberis, North Wales, for permission to use the frontispiece image; and last but by no means least my family and relatives who appear in lots of the pictures. Thank you!

Nigel Shepherd
North Wales
July 2008

1 THE BASIC KIT

The sport of rock climbing has come a very long way since its humble beginnings, widely acknowledged to be the ascent of Napes Needle in the English Lake District in 1886. The modern climber has all manner of safety protection that their counterparts in days gone by could never have dreamt of.

Not only is the sport considerably safer but it is also more accessible. There is no doubt that the development of indoor climbing venues has much to do with this. Climbing on an artificial wall is something that anyone can try – it doesn't matter what the weather is doing outside and a quick hour or two of practice can be snatched at almost any time of the day.

Like any sport requiring safety equipment, the level of security provided is dependent entirely on the individual's ability to assimilate instruction and to then implement it. Thankfully in rock climbing such procedures are relatively straightforward and a basic knowledge of the correct techniques, coupled with an understanding of the hazards involved, will lead to lifetime of rewarding experiences. Hopefully, this book will give you the basic knowledge you need to climb safely and inspire you to get out and climb more.

STYLES OF ROCK CLIMBING

The techniques in this book are geared towards beginners' climbing. To begin with it will help to understand the different styles of climbing. Essentially these are:

Indoor Climbing

The Manchester Climbing Centre, constructed inside a beautiful old church, is one of the foremost indoor venues in the UK. A good venue such as this will offer numerous climbs of all grades with fixed ropes in place for bottom roping, climbs with fixed protection for leading and bouldering areas where you can hone climbing skills without the encumbrance of ropes and other paraphernalia. Indoor venues are the starting point for many wannabe climbers and are accessible at any time of the year.

Top Roping

This style of climbing requires good access to the top of a crag and also good anchor points. The belayer on the right of the picture has walked around to the top, anchored herself to the rock and then dropped the rope down for the climber. The climber ties on and climbs up to the belayer. The belayer on the left of the picture has led the climb and has placed a directional runner to keep the rope in a straight line to the climber while she climbs the lower part of the ascent.

Bottom Roping

This is an instructional session in which two large groups are being entertained. The instructors have gone around to the top of the crag and arranged a complex web of anchors to provide several climbs for the group members. Ropes are attached to the anchors, which hang over the top of the short crag. The ropes run through a screwgate karabiner and, while one participant climbs on one end of the rope, the other is safeguarded by belayers who remain at the foot of the crag.

When the climber reaches the top of the climb, which in all cases is the karabiner securing the rope, they are lowered back to the ground.

This system offers several advantages over top roping – it is more sociable for group members and involves more people at any one time.

Trad Climbing

Derived from the word 'traditional', this is the purest form of climbing. A team of climbers arrives at the foot of their chosen climb, ties on to the rope and ascends the rock face, usually in stages, placing protection and arranging anchors on convenient ledges or 'stances' during the ascent.

This style of climbing requires those involved to have more than a basic knowledge of belaying and tying knots and requires considerably more equipment.

Sport Climbing
This is basically a ready-made climb for which all protection is in place. Normally this is done by the first ascentionist drilling holes in the rock. In each hole a bolt anchor is inserted, which has a hanger into which a karabiner and quickdraw can be placed and the rope clipped in for protection of the leader, who is first to ascend. It is a very popular style of climbing, requires little in the way of equipment and is usually only single-pitch. On arriving at the top of the climb the leader will thread their rope through an anchor point and then get lowered by their partner back to the ground.

There are several sport climbing venues dotted about the UK and thousands in mainland Europe, often located in stunning places, many close to easily accessed airports and beaches.

THE EQUIPMENT

All you need to begin rock climbing (both indoor and outdoor) is a pair of specialist rock shoes, a harness, a belay device and karabiner and the most essential item of kit – a rope.

Many indoor climbing venues have climbs where the rope is already in place for you to use, so to begin with such an expense might be unnecessary. However, once you progress to leading climbs you will need to have your own rope, even at indoor venues.

CHOOSING FOOTWEAR

Although this book is about safe rope techniques to use for climbing, a brief word about choosing the right footwear may be appropriate.

There are essentially two styles of rock climbing shoe: shoes that are desperately tight and uncomfortable for anything longer than 10 minutes and those of the comfortable variety that can be worn for much of the day.

An 'all-day' climbing shoe. These come in many shapes and sizes from numerous manufacturers. All climbing footwear has a smooth 'sticky' rubber sole that offers very good grip on dry rock and techniques of climbing take full advantage of the sticky rubber. An all-day style of shoe is perfect for starting out climbing. Make sure that it fits snugly but don't cram your toes into the end. Consider getting a size that allows you to wear a trainer sock inside for comfort.

A tight-fitting, precise and shaped shoe is desirable for difficult climbing where footholds are small and climbing techniques require complex body positioning and movement.

Comfortable shoes are clearly the preferred choice when starting out and the styles vary only between a Velcro closure or lace-up, and between a boot style and a shoe style.

A technical lace-up shoe. For more precise footwork you'll need a shoe that fits a bit tighter than something you might want to spend a whole day in. Normally you'll wear it quite tight without any socks so take time to choose something suitable.

There are many manufacturers offering differing styles – too many to mention here but the pictures here illustrate the main choices available. Many indoor venues offer a rental service for shoes so if you don't mind hiring it can be a significant cost saving initially.

A technical velcro shoe. This type is often preferred by climbers who want a really tight fit and one that is easily adjusted – mainly to relieve the agony of wearing them tight for increased technical performance. It is often said that you should buy a shoe two sizes below your normal foot size. However, this is not a good idea for those just starting out.

CHOOSING A HARNESS

Essentially, there are two styles of harness available: those that are a fixed size and those that are (almost) infinitely adjustable.

Those of the first type are generally lightweight and afford a high degree of movement appropriate to pure sport climbing when cumbersome equipment is not normally carried. Harnesses that are fully adjustable are much more suited to climbers who participate in a wide range of climbing disciplines, including winter and alpine climbing, when clothing requirements dictate fatter legs and waist on some days and thinner on others. These also tend to feature more generously padded leg loops and waist belt.

Similar to climbing shoes, there are numerous manufacturers offering a variety of styles.

The important parts of the harness in terms of safety are the belay or abseil loop, the buckles and, of course, the tie-in loops for the rope.

A fully adjustable sit harness. It is important to buy a harness that features some form of padding around the waist and around the legs. Almost all harnesses have a fail safe buckle system and the manufacturer will provide information on how to secure the buckles. This harness has adjustable leg loops as well as waist and is suitable for climbers who think their weight might fluctuate or for occasions when you might wear more clothing than on others.

A fixed-size harness. If you decide to buy a harness with fixed size leg loops you must make sure that it is a good fit. Nearly all harnesses have a stitched loop that connects the leg loops and waist belt together. Throughout this book I will refer to this as the abseil/belay loop. This loop is always through the same parts of the harness that you should thread the rope through when tying on for climbing. Individual manufacturers provide full safety instructions with each harness and you should always read these carefully and follow them to the letter.

CHOOSING A BELAY DEVICE

This is a key piece of safety equipment – without a belay device it will be very difficult to safeguard your climbing companions if they fall. In the early days of climbing body belays such as the shoulder belay and latterly the waist belay were used. These can work but are nowhere near as effective as a 'mechanical' belay device. There are friction-creating knots that could be used, but in normal climbing scenarios these are considered less appropriate.

Along with the belay device it is necessary to have a large round-ended screwgate karabiner. Often referred to as 'pear-shaped' or 'HMS', this type of karabiner is preferable because it will allow the rope to run freely, causing you less troublesome rope antics when paying out or taking in the rope.

The VC Pro. This is an excellent all-round lightweight belay device that features a notched groove for the all-important controlling rope to run through, making it easier to hold the weight of a falling climber. You must always use a large round-ended screwgate karabiner in conjunction with this styel of belay device as it allows the rope to run smoothly when needed.

The ATC XP, similar to the VC Pro. Almost all belay devices of this type feature two holes, each capable of taking the various diameters of rope. When you want to hold the weight of a climber on the rope you lock the controlling rope off by increasing the angle and gripping the rope tightly.

The grigri. This is a self-locking device: the rope jams inside it when a load is placed on the rope. They are great to use for indoor and sport climbing as they offer a high degree of safety in inexperienced hands. They can be slightly awkward to operate until you have had some practice using them.

THE ROPE

Ropes come in various sizes. Normally for single rope climbing you will use 11mm or 10.5mm diameter. There are some ropes of lesser diameters that are classified for use as single rope but they are more specialised. For double rope climbing 9mm is commonly used as is 8.8mm. 8mm is used for twin rope techniques and anything thinner is classed as accessory cord and is used for a variety of applications such as prusik loops or for threading on to nuts that are not wired.

To begin with you may not need to purchase a rope. Many indoor venues have ropes already in place for bottom roping and for other venues and uses you may be fortunate enough to have friends who will provide ropes.

Soon after starting out though you will need to bite the bullet and buy yourself a rope.

A 10.5mm diameter rope will suffice for all your early adventures out on to the rock or leading at indoor venues. There are too many brands to mention here and my guess is that final choice will be driven largely by price. Don't expect them to be cheap – most ropes are reassuringly expensive.

If you have a choice of length of rope it's probably better to go for a 60m (197ft) rather than a 50m (164ft) or 70m (230ft). You'll find that the suggested length is well suited to all styles of climbing described and particularly for sport climbing venues where many recent climbs are 30m (98ft) long.

THE REST OF THE KIT

Having acquired the basic kit the purchase of the remainder will depend largely on a number of factors including:

• How much climbing you aspire to do
• What style of climbing you will do most frequently
• Who you will climb with

For example, you may decide that your penchant lies entirely with indoor climbing and that all you might need to add is a rope long enough to be used at the indoor wall.

You may decide that you are only going to do sport climbing, where all the protection is afforded by pre-placed drilled bolt anchors. For this, all you'll need to add are a rope, a 60m (197ft) single rope, ideally, and a bunch of quickdraws (see following page).

If you want to climb traditionally protected climbs outdoors (known as trad climbing) you'll need to buy all the above plus a selection of crack protection devices (nuts and cams), some slings and a few more screwgate karabiners.

It's quite probable that you will team up with someone who has similar interests, even better someone who has all the gear already! If they don't have the kit you could agree to share out the costs and each purchase particular items to make up a full set of kit.

Collectively, all this equipment is referred to as the 'rack'.

The rack. This is the collective term used to describe all the equipment you carry for trad climbing. Needless to say it can be quite a heavy load! A variety of protection equipment is necessary and the selection of this equipment will depend very much on what level of climbing you undertake and how long the climbs are.

QUICKDRAWS

Quickdraws are short slings with a snaplink karabiner attached to either end. They are used for clipping into pre-placed anchors, such as bolts, and for extending wired nuts used for crack protection.

Your selection will be determined largely by price and the only other choices you need to make are between wiregate karabiners or solid gate, and the length of the quickdraw sling itself.

Wiregate karabiners are lighter. On their own the weight difference is insignificant but faced with having to carry a dozen or more on gear loops on your harness and possibly other equipment too, the weight saved can be considerable.

If you choose solid gate karabiners for each quickdraw, make one a straight gate (for clipping to the bolt or wired nut) and the other a curved gate karabiner for ease of clipping in the rope.

A good number of quickdraws to start out with would be ten, and you can buy more as you gain experience and find that you need them.

Quickdraws come in various lengths. Each quickdraw has a karabiner attached at either end through a sewn loop. The picture shows wiregate karabiners (above) and more standard snaplink karabiners (below). The curved gate karabiner makes it considerably easier to clip a rope in.

CRACK PROTECTION – NUTS

When you climb trad routes you have to arrange your own protection as you ascend the climb and to construct safe anchors to secure you and your companion to the cliff face (see Chapter 8).

Naturally occurring cracks and fissures in the rock allow the climber to place metal wedges or hexagonal nuts in these cracks and when a load is exerted on them they will, hopefully, tighten deeper into the crack. In order to cope with the natural variety in crack sizes and shapes a selection of different sized and shaped nuts is carried. Shapes of nut fit into two categories – wedge and hexagonal (usually with unequal sides, giving an 'hexcentric' effect). The climbing terms commonly used to describe this kit are 'wires' and 'hexes'.

A good selection to begin with will include a range of wedge-shaped nuts on wire from sizes 3 through to 10 and a selection of hexes 1 through to 8.

These are grouped together to form collections of small, (cracks narrower than your finger) medium (about finger width) and large (much wider than a finger). Hexes can be similarly split into two collections. Each group is carried on a single snaplink karabiner so that when you select a nut to place in a crack you have similar sizes to try all on the same bunch.

A selection of wedge shaped nuts are carried in groups according to size. Smaller sizes are solid metal and the larger are hollowed out to reduce the weight.

A selection of hexcentric shaped nuts. In some instances, hexes can be placed into nearly parallel sided cracks and a camming action under load will tighten it into the crack.

CAMS

Cams are magic devices that offer protection in seemingly unlikely places. A number of manufacturers produce cams but they are generically known as 'Friends' after the first type of device developed in the 1970s and still going strong to this day.

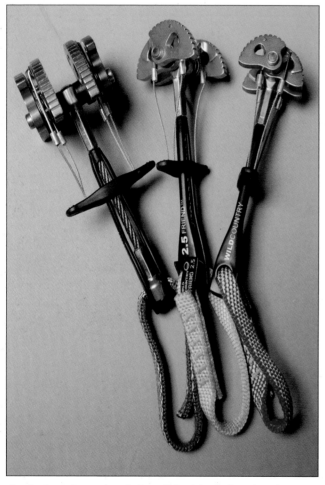

The mechanics of how they work are simple – each cam operates independently. They are fully closed by pulling the trigger, inserted into a crack and allowed to open until each cam bites against the walls of the crack. When a load is placed on the device each cam bites deeper into the rock giving increased security.

A placement should ideally be in a crack where the cams have space to open a small amount but not at the limits of fully closed or fully open.

A selection of camming devices. 'Friends' are the original camming device, designed by Ray Jardine. Other devices such as the Camelot and DMM 4cu and 3cu offer the climber a choice of styles.

SLINGS

A good basic rack will include about three long slings and a couple of shorter ones. These are often carried bandolier fashion slung over the shoulder but some climbers prefer to carry them tied up on a karabiner on the harness. Slings that contain an element of Kevlar (Dynema) are more durable than others available.

Tape slings are a very useful addition to the rack. They come in various lengths from short (60cm/2ft), medium (120cm/4ft) and long (240cm/8ft) and the ends are stitched together to form a closed loop. Two different widths are available (10mm and 12mm) and each is as strong as the other. The days of knotted slings are long gone. A rack will consist of a few medium slings, one long and maybe a couple of short ones.

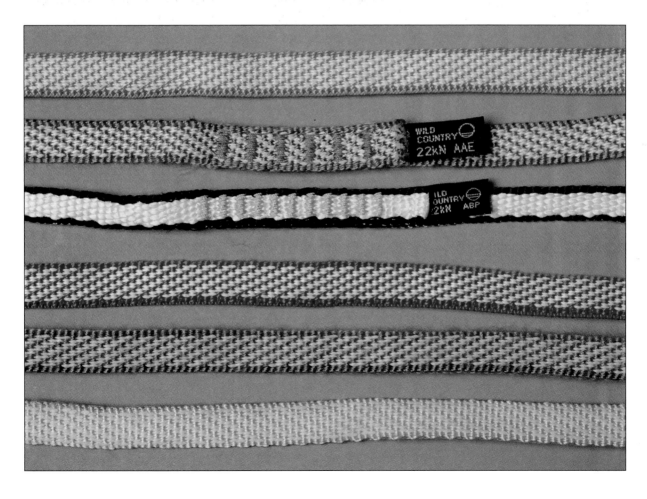

HELMET

Though not absolutely necessary for climbing, and certainly not for indoor climbing, a helmet is a desirable item of kit. At the very least it will protect your head from falling debris that might be dislodged by others at a crag venue and it might also go a long way to prevent serious injury if you are unfortunate enough to take a long fall.

There are several brands available each offering a few different styles. The main choice you'll need to make is between a polycarbonate shell or a cycling helmet style. In the end it's down to weight, comfort, fit and of course colour as a personal preference.

A good all-round helmet. A lightweight injection moulded polycarbonate shell helmet offers good protection and is durable. Helmets feature an inner adjustable cradle for a snug fit.

An ultra-light helmet made of expanded polystyrene, rather like a cycle helmet. Though probably not as durable as the model above, the feather weight of this helmet will be greatly appreciated. All climbing equipment suitable and approved for use in rock climbing will carry a CE mark and in some cases a UIAA stamp, which shows that it has been approved by an international body responsible for setting standards for climbing equipment.

MISCELLANY

A few extra screwgate karabiners for constructing anchors and a nut key for aiding the easy removal of jammed nuts from cracks are all that you might need to add to the rack initially.

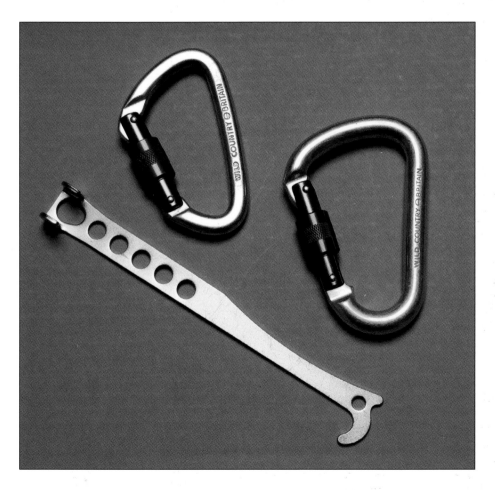

A nut key and a selection of screwgate karabiners. A nut key is used to assist the climber in extracting nuts placed in a crack that become a bit stubborn to loosen – an essential item of kit to help you save money.

The picture also shows a large round-ended screwgate karabiner, commonly know as a 'pear-shaped' or 'HMS' karabiner, and a D-shaped screwgate. For belaying and tying into anchors the HMS is essential and the D-shaped karabiner can be used for clipping ropes into anchors.

2 KNOTS

Thankfully, there are not too many knots you'll need to learn and those that are essential can be adapted to different situations. As you progress you may need to learn others but for the time being we'll concentrate on a few key knots.

THE FIGURE OF EIGHT

This knot is used mainly for fixing the end of the rope into a climbing harness.

There are two ways of tying it which are generally known as the 're-threaded' version and a 'double' version.

The re-threaded Figure of Eight is the most popular knot for tying the rope directly into the harness. It is very simple to tie and very safe if tied correctly.

The first step is to tie a Figure of Eight knot in the single rope about 90cm (3ft) from the end. (This suggested length will

The re-threaded Figure of Eight knot. It is used for tying in to a harness. Form a single Figure of Eight in the rope approximately 90cm from the end of the rope and thread the end through the harness tie-on loops.

Take the end of rope and retrace the line back through the Figure of Eight knot.

Follow the strands through until the end comes out of the knot. Try to get all the strands of rope to lie parallel to each other.

Finish the knot with a double stopper knot.

vary depending on the diameter of the rope you are tying it in. The figures are for 11 mm rope. Thinner ropes require slightly shorter lengths.)

The rope end is then threaded through the tie in loops of the harness as the manufacturer recommends. The knot is completed by tracing the end back through the single Figure of Eight. Try to make the ropes through the knot lie parallel to each other and make sure that the finished loop is neither too small nor too large. As a guide to the correct size you should just be able to get your fist through the loop.

The loop that is formed becomes a key part of the overall safety chain in climbing and will from now on be called the 'central loop'. We'll see later on how important this loop actually is.

Whenever you tie a knot in the end of a rope, you should always finish it off with the Double Stopper knot (see following page). In most cases this contributes negligibly to the strength of the knot but an enormous amount to the safety of the knot for it ensures that there is enough tail end of rope to absorb shock without the rope end pulling through the knot.

The Double Stopper knot should fit snugly up against the main Figure of Eight.

The finished loop that is formed should be about the same size as the belay/abseil loop – just large enough to squeeze your fist through. This is called the central loop.

The Double Stopper knot. This is an essential finishing off knot for many knots. It ensures that you have sufficient tail end of rope to prevent the knot unravelling if it is loaded during a severe fall or from working loose during the climb. Begin by spiralling the end of rope two times around the main rope, working towards the knot you are securing.

Having completed the two turns thread the end back through the loops that are formed, working away from the knot you are securing.

To finish the knot off correctly it should always butt up right against the knot you are securing.

An alternative way of finishing off the Figure of Eight knot is to tuck the end back into the knot. It requires less of a tail end of rope than a double stopper knot. Make sure that you pull the end fully through the knot to allow a minimum of about 50mm (2in) tail end.

THE DOUBLE FIGURE OF EIGHT

The Double Figure of Eight is used for attaching the end of the rope directly to the harness via a screwgate karabiner. This is handy for situations at the bottom of a short crag or indoor venue where the rope is threaded through an anchor at the top of the climb and the belayer stands on the ground to safeguard the climber (bottom roping). It makes changing the attachment from one climber to another much quicker and in some ways safer because once tied the knot is never undone.

The loop that is formed in the finished knot should ideally be big enough to squeeze two fingers through. Ensure that you finish it off with a double stopper knot. To tie on to the rope, clip in a large pear-shaped karabiner and

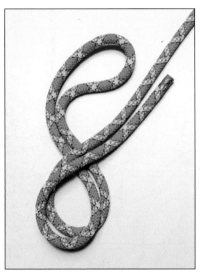

The Double Figure of Eight. Fold the end of rope back on itself to form two strands about 75–80cm (30–32in) long. This length is for 11mm diameter rope. Thinner ropes need less. Form a Figure of Eight as illustrated.

Thread the double loop through the first loop formed making sure that there is an 'eye' of rope loop large enough to squeeze two or three fingers through.

Pull the knot tight, finish with a Double Stopper knot and then clip the rope into your harness belay/abseil loop using a screwgate karabiner.

It is not necessary to clip the karabiner through the two tie in loops of the harness as the belay/abseil loop is quite strong enough. However if you insist on doing this try to avoid using the narrow end of an HMS or D-shaped karabiner to clip in. The illustration shows that the two tie in loops of the harness are bunched together in the bottom of the karabiner introducing a three-way loading on the karabiner, which could be dangerous.

If you need to attach via a karabiner through the two tie-in loops, use a large HMS screwgate and clip it in as shown.

then attach the karabiner to the belay/abseil loop on your harness. Finally, screw the locking gate up tight so that the karabiner cannot open accidentally.

Many climbers are under the impression that to clip in with a screwgate karabiner directly into the belay/abseil loop of a harness is not safe. The most common reason cited is that the belay/abseil loop is not strong enough. These people will instead usually clip a karabiner through the harness tie on loops, believing that this is better. Unfortunately it may not be a safe way at all of tying in to the majority of harnesses as it puts a load laterally on the back bar of the karabiner as well as longitudinally across the length of the karabiner. This problem is exacerbated if you use a small D-shaped karabiner and cram the harness into it.

THE BOWLINE

For the more traditionally minded climbers, the Bowline knot is another way to tie on to the end of the rope. When tying this knot many people use the 'rabbit out of a hole, around the tree and back in the hole again' technique. It is important to ensure that the 'tree' is the main climbing rope.

It can be tied into all harnesses with equal security.

It is particularly important to ensure that the knot is finished off with a Double Stopper knot. This should fit snugly right up against the Bowline knot itself.

Thread the end of the rope through the harness tie on loops and pull about 60cm (2ft) through. Form a loop in the main climbing rope as shown. This becomes the rabbit hole and the end of the rope the rabbit. The rabbit comes up out of his hole, runs around the tree . . .

. . . sees a farmer with a shotgun and dives back into his hole.

Pull the rope through the knot and tighten it until the loop that is formed is about the same size as the belay/abseil loop. Finish the knot off with a Double Stopper knot.

For extra security you can have the rabbit coming out of a double thickness hole if you wish. The double hole is formed simply by making an extra turn in the main climbing rope.

Finish the knot off in the same way.

THE CLOVE HITCH

Along with the Figure of Eight, this is the only other knot you are likely to need when first starting out. It is incredibly simple to tie and is used to secure yourself with the rope to anchor points.

This series of photographs shows how to tie the knot and tighten it once it is in place.

Form two loops as illustrated, pass the right behind the left and the two strands of rope you end up holding are clipped into a karabiner. When using the knot to secure yourself to anchor points you must use a screwgate karabiner. An HMS is best.

Impress your climbing buddies with this one-handed method of tying a Clove Hitch!

A COUPLE OF OTHER KNOTS

Two other knots are described below that might prove useful from time to time, particularly as you begin to climb more frequently and gain experience.

The Italian Hitch is a sliding friction knot and can be used for abseiling or for belaying in an emergency. The great thing about the Italian Hitch is that it can be used to take in the rope or to pay it out as it reverses itself when pulled in the opposite direction. The not so great thing about it is that it has a bit of a tendency to twist the ropes making them almost un-manageable.

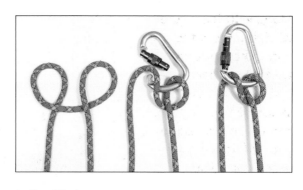

Italian Hitch
Form two loops as shown (just like the Clove Hitch), fold the two loops together – like closing a book, clip the two strands of rope you end up hold into an HMS screwgate karabiner.

The Double Fisherman's knot is used to join two ends of rope together. Occasions when you might need to use the knot include abseiling (see Chapter 6) and attaching rope slings to nuts. It consists of two double stopper knots tied in the ends of the rope around each other and pulled together so that they can't unravel themselves.

Double Fisherman's Knot
Lie the two ropes side by side and spiral the end of one rope twice around the other, working towards the end of the other rope. Thread the end back through the two loops formed and pull snugly tight. Spiral the other rope in a similar fashion but in the opposite direction to the first. Tighten both knots and pull the climbing ropes so that they stopper knots pull together against each other.

COILING A ROPE

There are three ways to carry a rope. The traditional method of coiling where the rope is coiled into loops and you sling it over your shoulder and put the opposite arm through the coils.

Before you begin to coil the rope run it through so that you have a neat pile of rope on the ground in front of you. Take the end that is on top of the pile and hold it in your hand so that the end is pointing towards you. Stretch both arms out to the side fully and form a loop which is held in the hand as shown. Repeat the procedure until nearly all the rope has been coiled.

When you have about 1.2m (4ft) left, fold the starting end of rope back on itself to form a loop on top of the coils.

Take the finishing end and wrap it tightly several times around the coils working back towards the loop formed in the starting end.

When you have about five or six turns thread the finishing end through the loop like this.

Hold the finishing end tightly with your thumb and pull the starting end through the whipping until it's tight.

The finished coiled rope can be carried over the shoulder.

Lap Coiling or Alpine Coils

When completed this method provides a handy way to carry the rope in much the same way as a rucksack.

❶–❸ *To begin, find the two ends of rope and pull both together to make a pile of rope on the ground. Begin lapping by holding the doubled rope about 75cm (28in) from the mid-point. Lap the rope as illustrated until you have approximately 1.7m (64in) left.*

❹–❻ *Hold the laps firmly and wrap the ends around the whole set spiralling up towards the hand. When you have made about four turns thread the ropes through as shown. Pull the loop right through and thread the ends through the loop. Pull the ends right trough and pull snugly to secure.*

❼–❾ *From the stage reached at ❹ you can finish off the coils in this way if you prefer.*

A lap coiled rope can be carried like a rucksack to make it more convenient.

Equipped to climb! Traditionally coiled ropes aren't so easy for little people to carry.

3 CREATING SOUND ANCHORS

If you climb only at indoor venues you'll not have to worry much about creating anchors. Neither will you need to be too concerned at sport climbing venues where the anchors and running belays are all normally pre-drilled bolts with double anchors in place for lowering off from.

Outdoors at trad climbing venues, whether you are leading a climb or arranging a top rope, you will need some basic skills and knowledge of how to arrange safe and sound anchor points.

There are a number of key pieces of equipment you'll need to create anchors and they can be conveniently divided into three broad categories.

It is a good idea to find somewhere easily accessible and not too far off the ground to practice placing protection equipment before you find yourself in a position where you need to do it for real.

NUTS

Nuts come in an enormous variety of shapes and sizes (see page 19). When placing any nut in a crack, do so with careful thought and an eye to where you anticipate the likely direction any load might come from. Make sure that there is plenty of rock surrounding the nut on two sides so that any load will tighten it in to the crack.

Make sure too that extracting it will be a relatively simple matter. You should also make sure that placements are well seated to prevent them being accidentally lifted out at a crucial moment.

A range of wedges can be carried to suit cracks from a few millimetres wide to about 4cm (1½in).

In order to construct sound anchors you'll need a rack of gear that is made up of a good selection of wedge-shaped nuts, hexes, a few cams if you can afford them and some slings.

 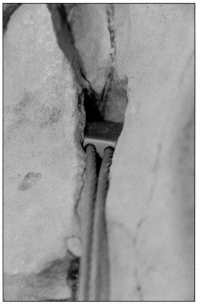

LEFT *A seemingly impossible placement can be achieved with a little ingenuity. Here the nut is placed sideways, then turned to fit perfectly in the shallow crack.*

BELOW *All nut placements should be seated firmly in place to prevent accidental dislodgement. A good way to do this is to leave the nut attached to the karabiner that you are carrying it on and take hold of the remainder of the bunch. By pulling downwards firmly the nut should seat itself positively.*

Almost exclusively wedge-shaped nuts such as 'rocks' from Wild Country, are purchased ready threaded with wire. It is possible to buy nuts that can be threaded with rope or tape but any nuts that take cord thinner than 7mm will be considerably less strong than the same nut threaded with wire. Wire nuts will often need to be extended to reduce leverage and the possibility that they might come out at an inopportune moment. Always extend wire runners by connecting the extension to the wire with a karabiner. Connecting with a sling directly around the wire is unacceptably dangerous. You may of course have to extend any running belay from time to time and the same theory applies.

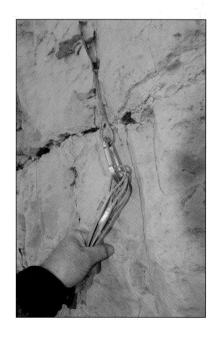

Hexcentric-shaped nuts are very versatile and can be placed in tapered cracks in addition to reasonably parallel sided cracks. When placed correctly the nut will twist tighter into the crack when a load is placed on it.

Nut placement is something of a science: study it carefully, practice lots and learn well.

Hexes can be used to great effect in almost parallel sided cracks. This placement illustrates how any load exerted on the sling attached to the nut will create a twisting or 'camming' effect, tightening the hex more securely into the crack.

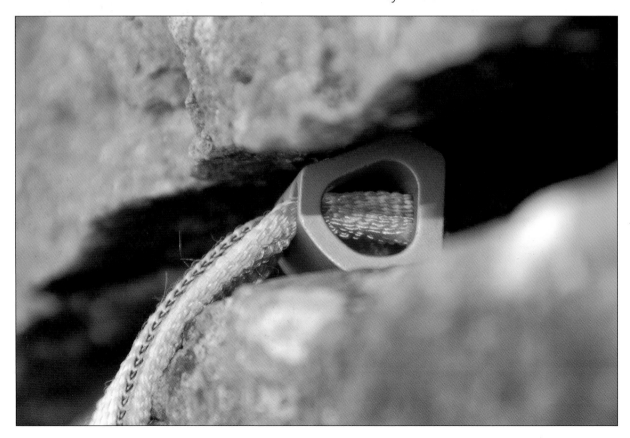

SLINGS

To use a sling is one of the oldest methods of anchoring used in climbing. You should only consider buying pre-stitched slings. They are much more convenient than the knotted variety. Unlike a knot the stitching cannot work loose or slip through itself.

Slings come in a variety of sizes from short 12cm (4½in) quickdraws through to massive 6m (20ft) 'cordelette' style slings and from ultra-light Dyneema (strands of Kevlar interwoven with nylon) to lightweight tubular tape and heavier super-tape. Slings can also be made out of rope, though this is much less common these days.

There are a few special considerations to take into account, of which the most important is that if using a sling draped over a spike or flake or threaded around a rock or tree, you must make sure that it is not stretched too tightly around the object. A sling placed in this manner is considerably weaker than one that has some slack in it. Make sure that there are no sharp edges that might cut into the material.

Slings have a variety of applications in rock climbing. Here a sling has been used to extend the anchor for a bottom roping setup over the edge of the crag. This is important at sandstone climbing venues such as Bowles Rocks in Kent – it helps to prevent erosion by ropes rubbing over the edge and creating big grooves in what is relatively soft rock. Slings are also used to wrap around trees, drape over blocks or flakes of rock or to thread around two rocks jammed together. Always satisfy yourself that any rocks you attach to are a solid part of the cliff face.

FRIENDS AND OTHER CAMMING DEVICES

The invention of 'Friends' and other similar camming devices has revolutionized protection for climbers. A well-placed Friend is as strong and reliable as a well-placed nut or sling around a spike. Like all gear they take a bit of practice to get used to. Take care not to cram the cams into a crack as they can be difficult, if not impossible, to remove.

Cams, such as Friends, provide opportunities for security where seemingly nothing is available. They work best in parallel-sided cracks that are suitably sized for the middle third of the full travel of individual cams. To place a cam, use the trigger to close the cams fully, place it in the crack and allow the cams to open up and bite into the sides of the rock. Any loading will force the cams open, thereby biting deeper and more securely into the rock. A cam that is jammed into too tight a crack may be a good placement but it could be difficult to remove because the cams cannot be closed any further. On the other hand, a cam placed with the cams almost fully open will be very insecure because the individual cams will not have sufficient movement to bite deeper into the rock. Such placements are likely to fail with even a light load.

METHODS OF TYING ON TO ANCHORS

Having described a variety of methods of creating anchors on the cliff face, we can consider the options available for securing yourself in order to belay a companion.

The methods can be split conveniently into the following categories:

1   The rope directly around the anchor or anchors
2   The rope attached to the anchor or anchors with a karabiner
3   The rope into multiple anchors brought to one central point
4   The anchor directly into the harness

We will consider each separately. Remember, without exception, that you should always be fixed tightly to your anchor and be standing or sitting in a position that anticipates the direction of loading.

If you allow slack in the tie off to the anchor you will be jerked forward until your weight comes on to the anchor and if you are off to one side of the anticipated direction of loading, you may be pulled sideways into the line of the loading if someone falls off. A combination of the two basic errors is often disastrous. Think carefully – it is an important aspect of the entire safety chain.

1 THE ROPE DIRECT

The rope can be looped directly over a block or spike of rock and the end secured to the harness with a Figure of Eight knot tied through the central loop. The rope could be secured equally well using a Clove Hitch into a karabiner or a Double Figure of Eight knot tied into a bight of rope and clipped via a karabiner into the central loop or tie on point. If you have more than one anchor point to tie into you must take the slack rope and repeat the process.

Using the rope to tie directly into anchors often takes up a fair length of the rope and so is not a method commonly used. It is most useful in situations where you have run out of gear or the block or flake you want to tie around is too large for a sling.

A simple way to secure yourself to an anchor point that doesn't require any other gear is to tie a variation of the Figure of Eight knot as shown. Take the rope from the anchor that you have clipped into and thread a double loop through the central loop of your tie in.

Form a Figure of Eight knot making sure that you have about 50cm (20in) of spare tail to the knot. Cinch it up tightly to ensure it doesn't work loose.

2 THE ROPE THROUGH KARABINERS ON THE ANCHORS

This is similar in some respects to the previous method. However, there are one or two subtle differences that make it much easier and more versatile.

The simplest way to secure yourself to the anchor is with a Double Figure of Eight knot tied in a bight of the rope or a Clove Hitch clipped directly in to a screwgate karabiner on the anchor. The drawback with this method is that if you have to stand out of arm's reach of your anchor, it can be difficult to gauge the correct length of the attachment in order to get tight to the anchor. My recommendation, therefore, is to attach yourself in this

One the easiest ways to tie to an anchor is to take the rope from your tie-in and secure it directly to the anchor using a Clove Hitch into a screwgate karabiner.

If you have to stand or sit out of arms reach of the anchor, clip the rope into the anchor screwgate, do the gate up tight and then clip an HMS screwgate into the central loop. Move into the belaying position you wish to take and then a Clove Hitch can be tied into this karabiner and easily adjusted to the right tension.

way only if you are within arm's reach of your anchor point. You will also find it an inconvenient method if you have to attach to multiple anchor points.

If you do have to move out of arm's reach of your anchor or anchor points, the system illustrated right is significantly more convenient. Take the main climbing rope and clip it into the first of the anchor karabiners. Don't tie a knot, just pass it through the karabiner. Screw up the gate. Take the rope back to a large pear-shaped or HMS karabiner which is attached to the central loop and secure it with a Clove Hitch or Figure of Eight. The locking Clove Hitch is more easily adjustable because it is attached to your harness.

To tie into a second anchor point simply repeat the same process. You could go on ad infinitum like this but

Yet another method of using Clove Hitches! If the second anchor is within arms reach of where you stand or sit you could clip directly to that anchor using a Clove Hitch.

If you have two anchor points it is possible to use the rope to attach to the second anchor using a second Clove Hitch secured to the HMS karabiner on your central loop.

obviously there comes a point where it would no longer be possible to get all the securing knots into one screwgate karabiner.

If both anchors are a long way from the stance, take the rope and clip it in to the first anchor. Then run it through a screwgate karabiner on the central loop, from there take it through the second anchor point karabiner. You now have a sort of 'M' shape of ropes which act like a pulley system. Use the friction generated to lower yourself back down to the stance whereupon you secure the rope that runs through the central loop karabiner and the rope that ultimately goes to your partner. It may of course happen that the second anchor point is within arm's reach. In this case you can tie into it directly with a Clove Hitch or Figure of Eight.

A word or two here about the use of screwgate karabiners on anchors. Whenever you attach a rope to your harness or central loop you should use a screwgate karabiner. Similarly you should use one for your main anchor attachment. Any secondary anchors could be connected with a snaplink provided that you assure yourself that it is safe to do so. Climbers tend not to carry enormous numbers of screwgate karabiners so if you do find yourself requiring the reassurance of a screwgate, and you don't have one to hand, rig up two snaplinks back to back or gates opposite as illustrated here.

If you have run out of screwgate karabiners, two snaplinks placed 'back to back' with gates facing in opposite directions is an excellent alternative.

Gates placed in opposition is another way of achieving a level of security with snaplink karabiners on anchors.

3. MULTIPLE ANCHORS TO ONE CENTRAL POINT

Often it will be convenient to bring two or more anchors to one central point of attachment. This can be done in a number of ways. One thing that you ought to consider whenever you connect multiple anchors to a single point is that if one anchor were to fail the load must come on to the secondary ones without any additional shock loading.

Two anchor points can be brought together into one point with separate slings if it so happens that the slings are of equal length. If they are not equal it may be possible to shorten them by tying a knot in the longest or extending the shortest.

There are four methods of using a single sling to bring anchors to a central point:

This photograph shows Clove Hitches tied at the anchor karabiners and at the central attachment point. The shock loading should one anchor fail will be negligible. It is possible to use this without the Clove Hitch at the central attachment point but you need to be certain that both the anchors are equally sound. This would give you the advantage of being able to change position on the stance yet maintain an equal loading on both anchors.

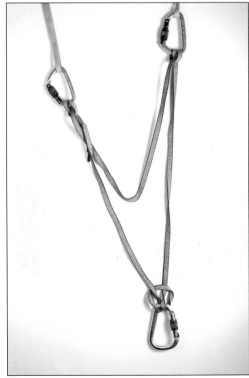

Using a sling to bring two anchor points to one central point.

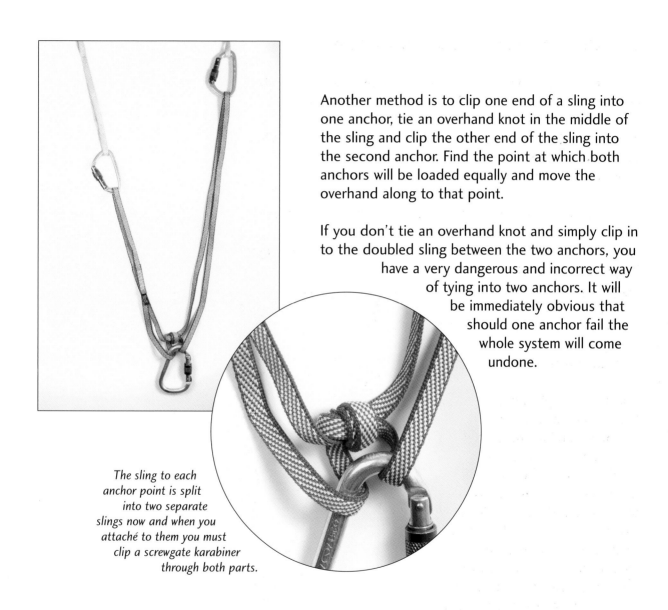

Another method is to clip one end of a sling into one anchor, tie an overhand knot in the middle of the sling and clip the other end of the sling into the second anchor. Find the point at which both anchors will be loaded equally and move the overhand along to that point.

If you don't tie an overhand knot and simply clip in to the doubled sling between the two anchors, you have a very dangerous and incorrect way of tying into two anchors. It will be immediately obvious that should one anchor fail the whole system will come undone.

The sling to each anchor point is split into two separate slings now and when you attaché to them you must clip a screwgate karabiner through both parts.

Two anchor points can be brought to a central point with a twist in the sling. This is quick to rig but if one anchor fails you cannot avoid a shock loading on the other. This method is useful if you are 100 per cent sure that both anchors are equally sound.

The fourth method uses up quite a length of the sling so make sure that you only use it when the two anchors are relatively close together.

Finally, many climbers carry very long slings called cordelettes and these are useful for attaching several anchors to one central point. They will be particularly useful for arranging bottom rope systems or setting up a practice anchor abseil.

This method is called the 'rolling equal', as wherever you stand or sit or place a load each anchor will be under equal tension. The twist in one strand of the sling is vital to prevent the screwgate karabiner sliding off the sling if one anchor should fail.

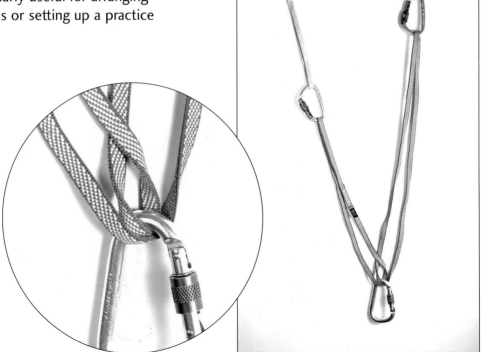

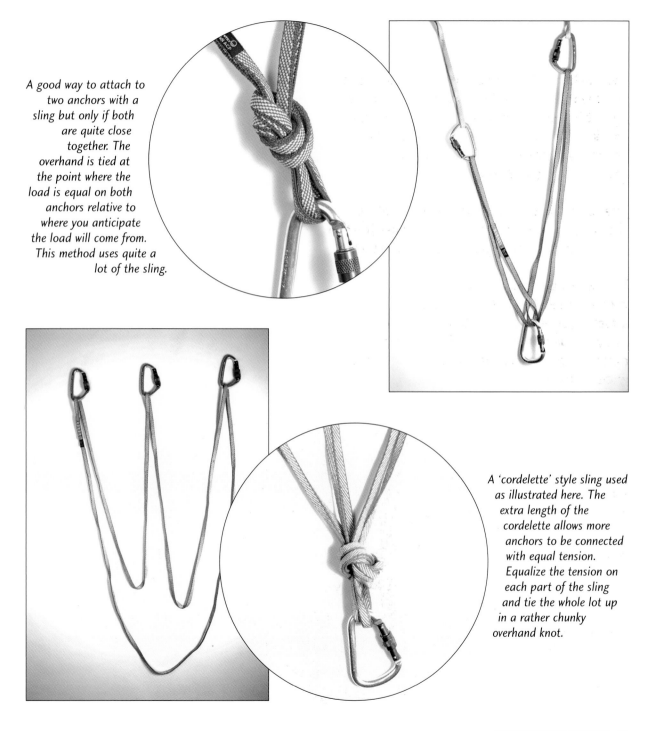

A good way to attach to two anchors with a sling but only if both are quite close together. The overhand is tied at the point where the load is equal on both anchors relative to where you anticipate the load will come from. This method uses quite a lot of the sling.

A 'cordelette' style sling used as illustrated here. The extra length of the cordelette allows more anchors to be connected with equal tension. Equalize the tension on each part of the sling and tie the whole lot up in a rather chunky overhand knot.

4. CLIPPING IN DIRECTLY TO THE ANCHOR

There is very little to be said about this method except that it is obviously very convenient should the occasion arise.

The only occasions where this is safely possible outdoors are when your main anchor is a sling around a block or flake of rock or is threaded between two rocks or around a tree. At indoor venues a sling is often used to connect to ground anchors directly.

You'll need to be sure that the spare length of sling available is a convenient length and that that length coincides with the exact position you wish to stand or sit in.

If an anchor is easily connected using a sling clipped in directly to the belay/abseil loop of the harness or into the central loop formed by your tie in it is very convenient to clip in directly. Here the belayer has attached directly to a ground anchor at an indoor venue.

4 BELAYING

When you've tied in to the end of a rope and are ready to start climbing you need to make sure that your partner is holding the other end of the rope securely so that if you fall you are unlikely to slip very far – in fact apart from a small amount of stretch in the rope you shouldn't fall any distance at all. The exception to this general rule is when you are leading a climb, which we will cover in some detail in Chapter 8.

BOTTOM AND TOP ROPING

To do this safely your companion needs to hold the rope through a belay device.

For simplicity we'll deal with only two belaying scenarios for the moment. One, bottom roping, is used at indoor climbing venues where the ropes are already in place or at an outside venue where you choose to rig up an anchor at the top of the climb and the rope is used through a karabiner attached to the anchor, draped over the edge so that belayers can stand on the ground. In both cases the climber is belayed up the climb and then lowered back down when they reach the anchor at the top.

The second scenario, top roping, is where the belayer will be anchored to the top of a climb and will drop the end down to the climber who will then be belayed from above as they ascend.

Having rigged anchors at the top of the climb the rope is doubled through the anchor and dropped to the ground. The climber ties on and the belayer puts the other side of the rope through a belay device. To belay safely it's a good idea to have somewhere flat to stand and have plenty of space for other group members to help with sorting out ropes or acting as a back-up belayer. At an indoor or artificial venue ropes are already in place for bottom roping.

Top roping outdoors requires a similar anchor set up to that for bottom roping but the main difference is that the climber is belayed from the top. You need to tie yourself in to anchor securely, ideally positioned at the edge of the crag where you can look down to watch the climber you are bringing up. The belay device is attached to the central loop so that any load can be shared between yourself and the anchor you are tied to.

BELAYING DEVICES

There are a number of different belay devices available, some with fancy names like Air Traffic Controller, Sheriff (because it arrests) and Grigri, and others with less flamboyant tendencies but equally practical.

Whichever one of the devices you decide to use the principles of operation are essentially the same. The rope is threaded through the device as the manufacturer recommends and is then connected to the abseil/belay loop of the harness or the central loop if you are tied into the end of the rope directly.

The part of the rope that goes directly to the person climbing is called the 'live rope' and the rope that comes out of the other side of the belay device is called the 'dead' or 'controlling' rope. The basic principle of safety lies in never letting go of the controlling rope and if you want to hold a load you lock the device off by creating a sharp bend in the rope.

The belay device can be clipped to the belay/abseil loop for bottom roping scenarios. Always use an HMS screwgate karabiner in conjunction with a belay device and make sure that the 'controlling' rope is not twisted and can be locked off by pulling it downwards.

The correct way to attach a belay device for top roping. It is clipped to the central loop with an HMS screwgate karabiner. The 'controlling rope' should always bee operated on the same side as the ropes go back to the anchor. In this case the left hand will hold the controlling rope.

A safe taking in procedure. The same method is used for belaying a climber in bottom roping and with any belay device, including the grigri. The basic principle is to **never** let go of the controlling rope. The hand that holds that rope is only allowed to hold that rope but the other hand is allowed to hold either rope.

From the starting position at ❶, grip the ropes and pull towards your body with the left hand and push away with the right. Reach as far down the rope as you can with the left but don't over-stretch.

Lock off the controlling rope with the right hand.

Take the left and grip the controlling rope in between the device and the right hand. Don't let go with the right hand!

Move the right hand to a position in between the device and your left hand

Go back to ❶ and begin all over again. When you do this for the very first few times it requires a certain amount of dexterity. If the climber is moving quickly it will be difficult to keep up with them so ask them to slow down. When using the system for taking in whilst bottom roping it is helpful to pull ropes through by pulling up towards where the rope is coming from.

BOTTOM ROPING

There are a number of important considerations to account for when belaying a climber from the ground.

Firstly ensure that the weight disparity between climber and belayer is not too great. A light person belaying a much heavier person is not a good combo but vice versa is ideal!

A light person may need to be anchored to the ground to ensure that they don't get pulled upwards by a falling climber. At indoor venues you will often find heavy bags of sand with a sling attached that can be clipped into the belay/abseil loop on the harness or anchors fixed into the ground. Outside venues will not offer such a simple solution and you may need to construct an anchor from available sources on the ground or even consider attaching another person as the anchor.

Weight differences between climbers can be a significant issue.

FAR LEFT *A simple way to attach a belayer to an anchor for bottom roping is to fix a sling to the anchor point and to attach the other end of the sling to the belay/abseil loop using a screwgate karabiner.*

LEFT *Whether you are bottom roping or belaying a leader outdoors you should try to attach yourself to an upward pulling anchor. In this picture the belayer has attached to a soundly placed nut. You can tie into the anchor using any of the methods described on pages 46–8, whichever is most appropriate for the situation you find yourself in.*

Another consideration should be how far you position yourself away from the base of the climb. Ideally you should only be a few feet out from the base so that when a load comes on to the rope from a falling climber or when you are lowering the force will not pull you into the crag. If you stand more than a few feet out from the base and an unexpected heavy loading occurs, you could easily get pulled off your feet and into the rock face. In the process there is a chance you could let go of the rope accidentally with dire consequences.

You must always pay close attention to the job you are doing. Idly chatting with mates near by and sloppy technique when taking in the rope could easily cause an unnecessary accident. Communicate regularly with the climber and ask how they are getting on, maybe point out some crucial hold that they might not be able to see and generally shout encouragement to say you have them securely on the rope.

An ideal position for the belayer to stand when bottom roping is close in to the base of the crag and slightly off to one side of the climbers line. A back-up belayer is on hand to assist should any problems occur.

Keep the rope snug at all times. This means that it should be tight without pulling them up the climb and the climber can feel the security of the rope there at all times. If you inadvertently allow a loop of slack rope to develop it's possible that a considerable force might be generated if the climber were to fall. There is also the possibility that they may injure themselves during the fall.

When a person is belaying for the first few occasions it's a great idea to have a back-up belayer holding the controlling rope as well. This person only needs to hold the rope loosely but does need to be alert enough to a fall situation where they can be ready to hold the rope if the belayer has difficulty doing so.

The back-up belayer need only hold the controlling rope lightly but does need to be vigilant and ready to help if the need arises.

TOP ROPING

This is a slightly more complex way to safeguard a climber and in a group situation much less sociable. The belayer will need to construct a good anchor at the top of the crag, usually tie into the end of the rope and attach themselves to the anchor using any appropriate method.

In addition to the important considerations outlined previously you'll also need to be particularly attentive to some other fine detail.

Firstly make sure that you are tightly attached to the anchor point. The rope or sling that secures you to the anchor must not have any slack in it at all. If you have to hold the weight of a climber you should be able to allow some of the load to pass directly through the belay device and on to the anchor behind you. Any slack in the system will not allow this until you have been pulled forward enough that the rope does finally come tight. By the time this occurs you may be dangling over the edge of the crag.

Secondly ensure that you are in line with the anchor. If you draw and imaginary line from the direction where you expect the load to come from back to the anchor point, ropes or slings that secure you to anchor must be a continuation of this line. Failure to observe this simple safety fact could result in you not holding the climber securely on the rope because you are struggling to prevent yourself being pulled off to the side.

One final point to bear in mind is that you should be able to see the climber coming up towards you throughout the climb. This will enable you to anticipate moves upwards, shout encouragement and point out holds to aim for with feet and hands.

The procedure and safety principles for taking in the rope are exactly the same as for bottom roping. The only slight difference is that you will have to have thought carefully about where you will put the spare rope as the climber ascends.

When you belay a climber from the top of a cliff or outcrop you will need to be as close to the edge of the climb as possible. In order to do this safely you must arrange an anchor, or anchors, well back and ideally slightly higher than your desired position. When you secure yourself to the anchor make sure that the ropes to the anchor are tight. You can then lean out safely over the edge to communicate with the person who is climbing the pitch and without fear of being dragged over the edge should they fall off.

LOWERING THE CLIMBER BACK TO THE GROUND

Lowering a climber once they arrive at the top of the climb is about communication and control.

The first thing to do is to lock off the belay device. Ask the climber to put their full weight on to the rope and when they have done so you can shout up that you are ready to begin lowering.

Start off nice and slowly so that the climber doesn't become too alarmed by a sudden downwards motion! They will soon tell you if they are going too fast.

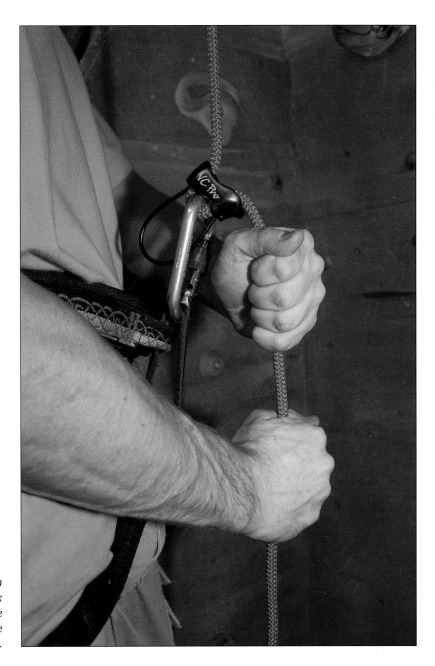

Lock off the rope and hold it with both hands. You can also lean back slightly against the rope once the climber has their full weight on the rope.

Keep two hands on the controlling rope for extra security and either allow the rope to slide slowly through your grip or feed the rope through the belay device. Your choice of technique will depend largely on what type of device you are using and the weight of the climber being lowered.

Try to keep the rope running smoothly and at a constant speed rather than a jerky stop-start lower. It will take a little practice before you become totally at ease with lowering – and being lowered for that matter.

If, at any time, the climber asks you to stop or slow down it is in both your interests to comply.

Lowering should be smooth and constant and the belayer needs to be alert to instructions from the person being lowered. The rope can be fed through the belay device rather than slid through the hands. By doing this you will always have good control over the lowering process.

SELF-LOCKING BELAY DEVICES

There are some belay devices on the market that lock up automatically when a load is placed on them. That's the theory anyway! In practice they will lock most of the time but there are occasions where they might not.

A self-locking belay device sounds very attractive to beginners particularly as it will surely take away the worry that they might not hold a falling climber.

In reality it is safer to assume that auto-locking can only occur if all basic safety principles are followed. Therefore techniques previously described are equally applicable to these types of devices.

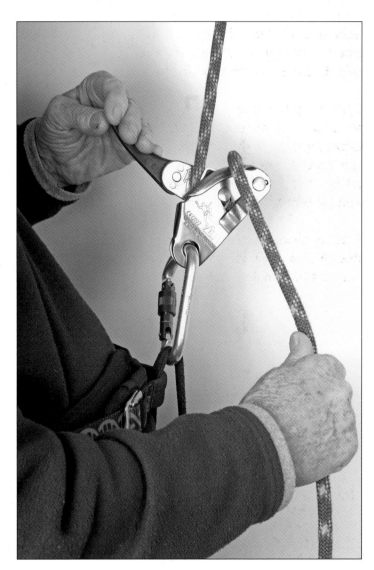

*Using a grigri to lower. The grigri will lock automatically once the climber has their full weight on the rope. Once locked you can release the grip of the device by pulling back on the handle and curling the controlling rope over the rolled edge of the grigri. Lowering is a subtle combination of handle release and grip on the controlling rope. **Never** lower a climber using only the handle release – you will lose control very quickly and the climber may hurtle at high speed towards the ground. Quite often you only need to pull the lever back a tiny fraction to allow the rope to begin sliding through.*

5 SAFETY

Safety when climbing is paramount. A momentary lapse of concentration could have serious consequences. Think carefully about the anchors that you arrange, always check and double check to see that knots are tied correctly and that belay devices are being used in the way that the manufacturer recommends, and be sure to secure your harness buckle. Remember that safety is a team effort and everyone involved must play their part.

INDOOR VENUES

It is tempting to think that indoor climbing is about as safe as you can possibly get in a potentially hazardous sport and to a large extent you'd be right to assume this.

There are, however, unfortunate incidents that cause injury to either climber or belayer or even to casual onlookers. In nearly all cases such incidents could have been avoided by careful consideration of some basic safety principles.

Some of the following suggestions may quite possibly be helpful, if rather obvious, and encourage you to climb considerately and with greater security. All are equally applicable to outdoor climbing too.

Always check that you are tied in correctly before you set off on a climb. It's very easy to become a little blasé about tying in, especially when you've done it hundreds, maybe thousands of times. If you are clipping in with the rope or auto-belay directly to a karabiner check that the karabiner is clipped to the correct part of the harness and that the screwgate is secured tightly.

When tying the rope into the harness tie-on points make sure that it is threaded through the correct parts of the harness and that the knot is correct.

If you use an auto-belay device at an indoor venue be particularly careful to ensure that you are clipped correctly.

If you are climbing with someone with as much experience as yourself, or more experience, get them to check too.

Always check that you have the rope through the belay device correctly when belaying. It's often a good idea to do a little test before the climber sets off on the route. This can be done quickly by the climber pulling on the climbing rope as you lock off the device. This is a particularly useful test if you are using a device such as a grigri and will let you know if you have threaded the rope through correctly or not.

When belaying always retain a grip on the controlling rope so that you are ready to hold even an unexpected fall.

Pay attention to the climber you are responsible for. Don't get distracted by other climbers on the wall or casual conversations with mates alongside.

Many indoor walls have auto-belay devices in place. These are devices placed at the top of climbs that operate on an inertia reel. They have rope or tape which is wound inside the device as you climb up but when you put your weight on the end of the strop they automatically lower you down in a controlled manner. It is vital that you clip into these devices using a screwgate karabiner clipped directly into the belay/abseil loop of your harness. As you do not need a partner to belay you there is often nobody to check you are tied in correctly. Don't just check – double check!

When belaying a climber in a bottom rope scenario or belaying a leader, you should stand close to the base of the climb and slightly off to one side. Some indoor venues have a line outside of which you must not stand when belaying.

Stand in a sensible position, reasonably close to the foot of the wall, not several metres out where not only will you be in the way of other users but also may get dragged in towards the wall if your partner falls off. Some indoor venues have a demarcation line outside or inside of which you must not stand when belaying a climber.

Consider using a weighted anchor bag or clipping yourself in to a ground anchor. This is essential if there is a serious weight incompatibility between you and your partner.

During the climb, communicate with your partner. You can't do this easily if you are distracted by your surroundings, so pay attention! If you watch carefully you'll be able to see when your partner is having difficulties and you'll be in a position to provide comfort by tightening the rope slightly or saying something encouraging like 'Go for it – I've got you tight on the rope' or 'Give it a go – I've got you'.

If your partner is leading the climb, be particularly attentive. Try to anticipate when they are likely to need rope to clip into a quickdraw for protection. There is nothing worse for a leader than pulling up the rope to clip in to a runner than to get near to the clip and the rope suddenly goes tight. Often it can overbalance them or pull the rope from their grasp. The moment they have clipped the rope into the runner, pull the spare slack through the device (assuming they have clipped in above their head of course).

Communication is especially important when your partner reaches the top of the climb. If you're belaying them in a bottom rope scenario, lock off the belay device and then tell them to put their weight on the rope. Hold them momentarily until they tell you they are ready to be lowered and then begin lowering steadily at a constant speed rather than suddenly and jerkily.

If they are leading you'll need to wait for them to clip the rope through the lower-off at the top of the climb before you can take their weight on the rope. Usually the climber will shout down when they have done this and it's normal for them to say something like 'OK, take me'.

When lowering back to the ground make sure that you slow the descent down sufficiently towards the ground so that the climber doesn't land too heavily.

If you lead an overhanging climb and your partner wants to follow the climb on a top rope it is vital that you tie into the end of the rope that passes through all the quickdraws clipped on the ascent. The reasons for this ought to be obvious but it is often overlooked by inexperienced climbers. If you don't tie into the end of rope suggested and you fall off during the climb you will almost certainly swing out a long way from the wall. This is probably not too much of a danger to the climber – it is inconvenient – but it could be extremely dangerous for other users.

If the weight compatibility between you and your partner is not perfect consider attaching yourself to a ground anchor. Here the belayer is attached to a bag filled with sand. Note the attachment is directly to the belay/abseil loop. An alternative ground anchor can be seen in the photo on page 54.

At a busy indoor climbing venue, try to make sure that you keep the rope and your equipment in a reasonably tidy pile near to your feet. A rope bag or rope tarp is particularly useful for this.

OUTDOOR VENUES

The principles of safety relating to tying on to the rope, belaying and communication, apply as much outdoors as they do indoors. There are, however, several additional considerations to take into account when you are outside climbing.

One of the main considerations is probably objective danger from falling debris. Rocks can be dislodged by climbers or occasionally by

the rope and, very rarely, naturally. When climbing it will not be easy to get out of the way of anything that falls off and neither will it be too easy to move when you are belaying. It is sensible to wear a helmet for outdoors climbing. This will give you some protection and may also help prevent injury in a fall. A great many climbers choose not to wear a helmet and in truth it is ultimately down to a personal decision based on experience. As a beginner you may not have the necessary experience to make this kind of judgement and it is therefore highly recommended that you wear head protection.

Another important point to consider is the availability of anchor points. With the exception of sport climbing venues, outdoor venues will not offer much in the way of pre-placed anchors or protection. At a crag that is used frequently by instructional groups you may find pegs driven into the rock or stakes in the ground specifically placed for this purpose and strategically situated for particular climbs. Even though such anchors may be in place it is a good idea to check out their provenance by testing them before deciding to use them. The simple rule of thumb to apply is: if you are not satisfied they are safe or appropriate, **do not**

Any equipment that you find in place on the crag or at the top of the crag should initially be treated with caution. Check it out carefully and if you have the slightest doubt as to its provenance arrange your own anchors.

use them. The same rule will apply to anchors that you arrange yourself using natural features in the rock or trees or boulders or flakes.

If you set up bottom roping systems you'll ideally need to have the anchor draped over the edge and below the very top of the crag. Consider using some protection around the rope or slings to the anchor to prevent serious abrasion, both of the anchor itself and of the rock.

Where ropes or anchors run over a sharp edge or over abrasive rock try to protect the equipment using some sort of padded covering. Old bits of carpet are handy for this, or you can make or buy special edge protectors for this purpose.

6 ABSEILING

Abseiling is often seen as a fun activity in its own right and for many folk it has absolutely no connection to climbing whatsoever.

For the rock climber it is an important skill to learn and one that will become considerably more important as you progress.

STARTING OUT

It is a relatively simple matter to set up a practice abseil provided you have a suitable venue. Ideally try to find a short crag with good anchors at the top and one that has easy access to both top and bottom. If possible, find somewhere with anchor points above the edge of the crag. This will make starting off much simpler.

For your first few abseils you'll need to be attached to a safety rope so rigging the anchors for the session is relatively complex. In an ideal world you'll try to have a separate set of anchors for the abseil and another set for the safety rope belayer. If you only have one rope you can split it into two halves and use one half to abseil on and the other half as the safety. This will mean that you abseil on a single rope rather than a double. In 'normal' climbing scenarios you would abseil on a doubled rope threaded through an anchor so that when you reach the end of the abseil you are able to retrieve your rope by pulling on one end.

There are specific devices that can be used for abseiling, although a belay device will work perfectly well for abseiling either on single rope or double rope. You set up the rope in the belay device in exactly the same way as you do for belaying a climber.

The choice of location for a first abseil requires careful consideration. It should be accessible both from above and below and it needs to be a fairly low angle, say around 45 degrees. It should be a smooth open slab ideally and be blessed with sound anchors. The starting point for the abseil should be flat and easily accessed without risk of falling off the edge of the cliff.

Ideally anchor points should be at the back of the ledge and higher than waist height to facilitate ease of starting the descent. A venue that fulfils all criteria is perfect but hard to find – inevitably compromises have to made somewhere.

The figure-of-eight descender is a device specifically designed for abseiling. It can be used for belaying safety too but is nowhere near as efficient as a belay device, which also happens to be an excellent abseil device. For the first few abseils a figure-of-eight descender is a good tool to use as it provides excellent friction and control for the abseiler. However as a rock climber it is a good idea to move on to the belay device as soon as you can.

As with belaying technique the all-important rope is the controlling rope. You mustn't ever let go of it! If you do let go when you are abseiling without a safety rope or a safety back up you will fall very quickly to the ground.

The belay device is set up on the belay/abseil loop of the harness in exactly the same way as you would for belaying a climber. The rope that goes to the anchor comes out of the top of the belay device and the all important 'controlling rope' from underneath. The safety rope can be clipped into the belay/abseil loop either above or below the abseil device.

THE TECHNIQUE

It is important to maintain a good position while you are abseiling down the rock face. This means that your feet must be flat on the rock with your legs straight and your upper body slightly bent towards the rock.

In order to slide down the rope you'll probably have to push the controlling rope through the abseil device initially. Make sure that you lean back with all your weight rather as if you are having a tug of war with the abseil rope!

The most difficult part of any abseil is getting started. Once you are on your way it becomes considerably smoother. Simply walk backwards down the rock face and don't forget to look where you are going! It's not a great idea to do commando-style leaps down the crag. That particular technique is best left to commandos. It puts much less strain on anchors and is easier to control if you take a steadier approach.

A perfect abseiling position! Feet flat, legs straight and body slightly bent at the waist. As you let rope slide through the abseil device you can walk your feet down. In the beginning it's better to take small steps down but as you gain confidence and experience you can go faster.

SAFETY BACK UP

It is possible to set up an abseil using a failsafe back in case you do accidentally let go of the controlling rope or you are descending and need to let go in order to sort out ropes or retrieve equipment. It's better to practice this technique after you have had a few abseils using a safety rope.

If you are standing at the foot of an abseil and another climber is descending the rope you can provide a level of safety back up by holding the bottom of the abseil rope or ropes. If you pull hard on the ropes the person descending with come to a stop because no rope will slide through the device as you are effectively taking over the controlling ropes of the descent. Climbers will often look after each other on abseils like this. It's particularly useful when you have several abseils to make in order to descend a high cliff.

Using a safety back-up. When you have had a few abseils using a safety rope, and you feel confident to do so, it's a good idea to try without the safety rope. You could abseil with no safety back up at all but this is not recommended: if something were to go wrong it could prove catastrophic. A simple safety back system used by rock climbers is to attach a back up to the leg loop of the harness.

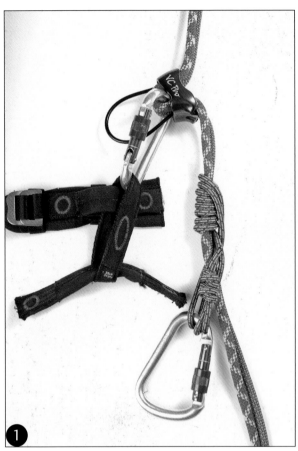

The set up for using a French Prusik safety back up. The abseil device is threaded with the ropes and then attached to the belay/abseil loop of the harness. Put a French Prusik (**❸**) on the controlling ropes and attach it to one of the leg loops of your harness. This has to be on the same side as you hold the controlling rope. As you descend you hold your hand over the French Prusik and slide it down the rope with your controlling hand. If you accidentally let go of the controlling rope, or deliberately of course, the French Prusik grips the controlling rope preventing further descent.

You may find it usueful to extend the abseil device away from the harness when using this safety back up system. Here a short quickdraw has been used. Note that screwgate karabiners are used at both ends of the quickdraw.

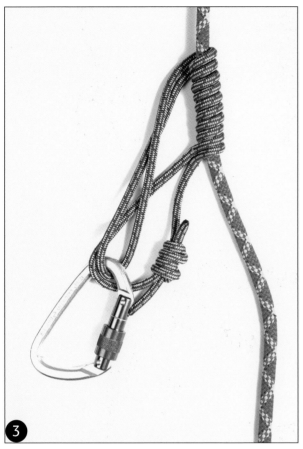

The French Prusik is one of a number of knots that fall into the category of 'Prusik' knots. These are knots that can tied around a rope and moved but when loaded in a particular direction they will lock around the rope they are tied to. You will need a short length of 7mm accessory cord to form the prusik loop. About 1.5m (5ft) should do the job. The loop is formed by tying a Double Fisherman's knot (page 33) To tie the French Prusik around the rope simply spiral it around as shown and bring the two ends together equally and attach a screwgate karabiner. This is then clipped to the leg loop of the harness.

A simple way to lock off an abseil if you do not use of French Prusik, regardless of which device you are using. This will stop your descent and allow you to use two hands to sort a tangle out in the abseil ropes or to retrieve equipment from the climb. Two turns is usually sufficient but three or four is more secure.

ALTERNATIVE SAFETY ROPE SETUP

A technique for operating the safety rope that will be found particularly useful if you take friends or family climbing allows you to stand 'outside' of the safety system.

If you are looking after a group of people, particularly children, this system will give you greater flexibility in terms of being able to move around and help people get set up on the abseil and to make the first tentative steps over the edge.

A system of operating the safety rope that does not limit the belayer to one position at the top of the crag is particularly useful if you are going to take friends or family out abseiling.

Instead of tying in to the anchor and belaying off the harness you clip yourself to the anchor using a sling or, as shown here, a snake sling with different attachment points. The safety rope to the abseiler can then be operated directly attached to the anchor using an Italian Hitch to secure the rope (page 33).

7 INTRODUCING FRIENDS AND FAMILY

If you are an experienced climber you may at some point want to introduce your friends or your family to climbing. Before you consider doing this be absolutely sure that you are confident you can do it safely. This assumes a good level of previous climbing experience and a sense of responsibility to ensure the safety of those you are looking after.

Increasingly one sees groups of friends, university groups and families at single pitch climbing venues where clearly there is a great deal of enthusiasm to introduce newcomers to the sport but all too often it is apparent that basic safety knowledge along with a misunderstanding of the principles of safely introducing beginners to the sport is lacking. Very occasionally it is not always clear who the day out is intended for.

It is tempting to suggest that introducing the sport to beginners should always be left to those professionally qualified to do so yet there are many thousands of climbers out there who have relied on friends and family to introduce them and who continue to enjoy their passion for rock climbing. It is an admirable way to take those first steps into the vertical (or slightly off-vertical) world.

This chapter offers some advice to anyone who feels able to introduce their friends or family.

PRINCIPLES

There are several principles to observe. First and foremost is that the pleasure for you will be seeing folk have fun, enjoy themselves and develop a yearning for more. If you see it as an opportunity to get some climbing in for yourself you will begin on the wrong foot and the day will be ruined from the start.

The day should ideally be planned carefully beforehand. Think carefully about the venue. Your choice of location will be determined by a number of factors and it is assumed that you will be climbing at a venue where you will operate a bottom roping system for simplicity and sociability.

How many are there in your group?

A large group of people will need quite a bit of space at the base or top of the chosen venue and a safe area to hang out at when not climbing.

Are they youngsters or adults or a mix of the two?

If you have young children you'll need to think about how you'll control them and keep them interested in what you are trying to achieve. It's particularly important that you keep youngsters involved and active for much of the time. You may not be able to allow them to wander off to explore on their own and will almost certainly need to set parameters defining where they can and can't go when not climbing or belaying. Adults, on the other hand, will need less structure and may be left to their own devices if given simple limits.

When you are sure that you have enough experience to take care of yourself you may wish to take friends and family climbing. A fun day out can be had even on a very short crag with good anchors and space to hang out beneath the climbing – even non-climbers can be involved if the venue is easy to reach. Clearly you need to be sure that the crag is free of objective dangers such as rockfall if everyone is going to remain so close to the foot of the climbs. Bottom roping belay systems are ideal in such a scenario.

Are they up to the task physically and emotionally?

It's simply not a great idea to push people who are not physically capable and neither is it a good idea to push folk beyond a threshold that tests their emotional limits. A sympathetic attitude is what is often required to achieve success, not the gung ho 'lets see what you're made of' attitude often witnessed.

What equipment do you have to provide?

A large group of folk will require several harnesses, helmets and screwgate karabiners, not to mention a few ropes for different climbs plus gear for rigging up suitable anchors. If you are only taking a couple of children or friends you'll require much less kit. Small children will need to use full body harnesses for safety.

What is the weather forecast for the day?

Dry, sunny and warm days are undoubtedly the best for introducing rock climbing! If the forecast is for a deluge during the day it might be prudent to call it off until the weather is better. Wet and slippery rock climbing is not the greatest of fun days out!

Small children benefit from a full body harness. It is considerably more comfortable for them, particularly when being lowered. It is also safer

Do you have prior knowledge of the venue?

If you are familiar with a particular climbing venue it will save a good deal of time when setting up ropes and anchors for climbs and in selecting appropriate climbs for novices.

A number of anchor points can be brought together using a rope. Two ropes for climbing on could be attached to the anchor, as illustrated.

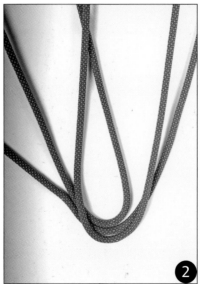

A good system for equalising tension to all the anchors.
❶ *Clip the end of the rope into one anchor and loop it back through a karabiner on your harness. Take it back to a second anchor and then again into your harness again. Repeat for the number of anchors you want to link and then holding the rope indicated move towards where the final position of the anchor needs to be placed.* ❷ *When you are in the desired position unclip all the ropes from your harness, fold the rope you were holding back towards the anchors and take hold of the bunch or ropes and tie them in an overhand knot.* ❸ *If you have several anchors the knot will be quite bulky. The karabiners to connect ropes should be clipped through all the ropes in the finished loop.*

Are you the only experienced climber in the group or are there others you could ask to help share the responsibility?
It is always helpful if there at least a couple of climbers prepared to share the responsibility. It means that one can focus on preparation while another can entertain the troops – particularly important for young family groups.

Is the venue easy to reach?
A venue within a short walking distance of where you can park is ideal. It means that if needed folk can get back to a safe haven quickly or if something goes wrong help can be called quickly.

This is a good venue for beginners in an old slate quarry where all the climbs have been equipped for sports climbing. You will need to lead these climbs in order to set up top ropes so someone who can belay you is an essential addition to the team.

Does it have safe areas at the top and bottom of the crag?

If you intend to do some abseiling it will be helpful if you select a venue that has easy access to the top of the crag and one that also has reasonably flat ground beneath with open areas where you can see folk at all times.

If you arrive at an empty crag first and set up ropes be considerate of other users and don't 'hog' the climbs all of the day.

Will it be busy on the day you intend to visit?

An odd consideration perhaps, but nevertheless one that could have an important influence on what climbs will be available to you during the day. Busy crags often mean certain climbs might be occupied for an entire day and that you might only be able to get on to one or two of your intended climbs. It is better, and more considerate to other users, not to dominate one particular area of a crag or specific climbs that might preclude others from using them too. There are few things

more irritating than to arrive at a crag to discover ropes hanging from several climbs while those who put them there are only using one or two at any one time.

Does the venue have suitable climbs for beginners?

Once again a rather obvious consideration but so often overlooked. It is important for novices to achieve success on their introduction to the sport. If they achieve this easily they will be encouraged to try more but if it is a life or death struggle they are not likely to want to try again. Finding a good balance between easy success and what might be considered a challenge will require a significant effort on the part of the facilitator.

Easy climbs for children and adult beginners are essential. It is important to achieve success without feeling too terrified. A small slab by the sea provided good climbing on this occasion. Though not a recognised climbing area such opportunities abound both at coastal locations and inland.

A variety of climbs available is a bonus. The easiest style of climbing will be found on low angle slabs but equally 'interesting' features such as cracks and chimneys will often provide good sport at the right level.

A SUGGESTED STRUCTURE FOR A DAY

Rock climbing is mainly about movement over rock, and the ropework and safety aspects, though integral, could be considered secondary. Understanding the principles of movement is a good way to begin. Find somewhere that has some easy bouldering near by. Anything low angled with an abundance of foot and handholds is ideal. For children particularly, moving over rock is a fairly natural activity so try not to constrain them with techniques that might be more appropriate to an adult who is less physically attuned. Fun and games are more the order of the day.

Children are often too light to belay each other and they may not even have the strength to pull the rope through the top anchor to take in safely. You could have one pulling the rope down, one pulling the rope through the belay device and one acting as a back up belayer. Including the person climbing that involves four people at any one time in the climb.

Do a few bits of ropework so that everyone understands the principles of safety essential to a safe day on the crag but again don't let technical aspects obscure the element of fun. One basic knot for tying on and techniques of belaying and lowering are the essential components.

An explanation, or better, a demonstration, of how the system works will pay dividends and make life simpler when it comes time to climb. Include some basic climbing commands but don't get bogged down with expanding on terminology. There will be plenty of opportunity for this whilst folk are climbing.

When you are ready to begin, get climbing as soon as you can.

A technique used by instructors that may be found useful is to involve a few people in the safety system. For children this is particularly beneficial. One can be attached to the belay device and pull down the climbing rope whilst another can pull it though the device and a third can act as safety back-up. This involves three or four in the climb all at the same time.

This suggestion requires the use of a particular belay device. Those that are suitable are the SRC from Wild Country, the grigri or a figure-of-eight descender.

The SRC (single rope controller) from Wild Country is an ideal device to use. It has an element of 'self-locking' about it when loaded but not in the same way as a grigri, and is easy to operate. Here we see the basic setup for two people to operate the belay device.

The basic principle of lowering a climber using the SRC is to keep the device in the 'locked off' position, pull back gently on the long arm of the device until you just feel the rope begin to slide. To slow down release the long arm, to speed up pull it back further. Do **not** let go of the controlling rope under any circumstances.

Sport climbs will require someone to lead the route first in order to set up a bottom rope. This may not be possible if there is no one in the group with previous experience of belaying.

Many indoor climbing venues have areas specifically set up for youngsters climbing.

If you intend visiting a sport climbing venue bear in mind that you may not be able to get around to the top of the climb to rig anchors and may have to lead a climb to rig a bottom rope system. If you don't have anyone in the party experienced at belaying a leader and lowering off it may not be possible to do this. There are only a few outdoor sport climbing venues in the UK that have easy climbs but there are lots in Europe that are specifically set up for this and even some climbs where the bolts are only a few feet

There are a huge number of outdoor venues in Europe where you can combine family beach activities with a bit of climbing. This is Cala Fuili in Sardinia and there are climbs from the very simplest that have lots of bolts to practise leading to the very hardest imaginable – enough to satisfy everyone.

apart to encourage children and nervous novices particularly to lead.

Indoor venues often have areas set aside specifically for youngsters to have a go at climbing. Alphabet holds, gnarly or smiley faces or animal shaped holds add to the fun. Adults are allowed too!

A family beach holiday can be combined with a bit of climbing too! Mixed activity holidays please all the family.

8 LEADING A CLIMB

Once the bug has bitten you there's no turning back! In extreme cases it becomes an all-consuming habit requiring constant feeding – be prepared!

The first signs that you are becoming addicted manifest themselves in the desire to lead a climb.

STARTING OUT

Indoors is as good a place as any to try your first lead climb, particularly if it's a venue you are familiar with. Most indoor venues have climbs equipped with closely spaced bolt runners and at a variety of easy grades specifically for this purpose. Similarly, outside sport climbing venues where all protection and lower-offs are pre-placed may feature easy climbs suitable for a first lead.

Outside trad climbing is something altogether different and you'll need a good understanding of how to place the assortment of protection devices available and how to arrange safe anchors at the top of the pitch or climb and how to bring up your partner. This is one aspect of learning the craft of rock climbing where a day or two of instruction from a qualified professional is really worthwhile. He or she will be able to climb alongside you offering advice on gear placements and how to arrange anchors on belay stances.

Sport climbing venues with pre-drilled bolts in place are ideal for early leading practice outdoors. Choose climbs that are relatively easy to begin with before progressing on to more difficult climbs. This spectacualy rock formation is at Capo Testa in northern Sardinia and though this is quite a difficult climb the area has a host of more straightforward options.

A classic climb in the truest sense of traditional climbing. This is the Direct Route on the Milestone Buttress in the Ogwen Valley, North Wales. To climb safely you'll need to develop skills of runner placement, anchor rigging and stance organisation. It is important to choose climbs of a low standard to begin with so that you are not physically and emotionally stretched.

Indoors you'll only need to provide a rope to lead climbs. You'll have everything else required which is only a belay device and karabiner. All the quickdraws will be in place for you to clip for protection. Outdoors at a sport climbing venue you'll need to provide your own quickdraws and you'll also benefit from having an extra screwgate karabiner.

Obviously a climb such as this requires an enormous amount of strength and good technique. When you learn to lead at an indoor venue you may progress quite rapidly but it is better to spend time on much easier climbs to learn skills of clipping runners and belaying technique when climbing outdoors.

Before moving on it's worth mentioning a few facts about belaying a leader. The forces involved in a fall are considerably greater than any you will have experienced when bottom roping or top roping. If a leader falls off, the person belaying needs to react quickly to prevent a longer fall than might be desirable. As a basic rule of thumb a leader fall will be about twice as long as the distance they are above a piece of protection that will stop them. Usually it is slightly longer because climbing ropes and the tie-in system introduce an element of stretch which acts as a shock absorber to some extent. Therefore a leader whose tie-in at the harness is 60 cm (2ft) above the point of protection should fall 120 cm (4 ft) plus a bit. However, given the same scenario but this time 3m (10ft) above the protection the fall will be 6m (20ft) plus a fair bit of stretch. In the first example the force felt by the belayer will be negligible but in the second example it will be considerable. Not only that, in a longer fall the leader will fall at higher speed and is much more likely to injure themselves.

An example of a leader fall. At the point that the leader fell he was approximately 4 or 5 feet above the runner but the second has quite a big loop of slack rope in front of him. This will greatly increase the length of the fall.

The slack rope begins to be pulled through the runners and the rope starts to tighten. At this point the second will begin to feel the load coming on to the rope and has a chance to prepare for it.

Finally the leader stops falling and the rope comes tight. The total length of fall is close to 20 feet and though the leader is clearly not going to hurt themselves it is a substantial distance to fall and places considerable forces on the belayer.

This is a fairly simplistic overview for there are other factors that might need to be taken into account but for now it serves as an example of what you might expect.

Ideally then a leader would place running belays (protection) at regular intervals, say every 150cm (5ft) or so. By doing this they will be able to climb with runners above their tie on point for much of the time. Routes at indoor venues are usually blessed with fixed protection every 120–150cm (4–5ft) so they are ideal for learning to lead. Outdoor sport climbing venues may not afford the same luxury and pre placed protection could be as much as 3m (10ft) apart or more in some cases.

It is nearly always a good idea to anchor the leader's belayer at the base of a climb. More so when a tree is conveniently situated at the bottom. The belayer or second should remain attentive to the leader's progress at all times.

YOUR FIRST LEAD

To set yourself up for your first lead, uncoil the rope at the base of the climb, tie on to the end of the rope by threading it through your harness tie on points and then using an appropriate knot – not via a screwgate karabiner. Consider whether or not you need belayers to be anchored at the base of the climb. Your partner will take the rope that is attached to your harness and put it through the belay device as normal. He or she is now referred to as the 'second'.

Here it should be readily apparent what will happen if the leader were to fall – a good soaking for the second as they get dragged sideways into the water! An anchor placed in the rock slightly behind the belayer would be an ideal way to prevent this.

if there are no anchors at the base of the climb or you choose not to use one, it is a good idea to sit on the ground. This is particularly important if the ground is rough or the ledge that you start the climb from has any kind of potential hazard.

The belayer will need to pay out enough rope so that it is not too tight between the two of you. Ideally a small loop of slack rope is sufficient to allow the leader freedom to move up. A good belayer will try to anticipate how much rope their leader needs to make moves up the wall.

When you reach the first point of protection you'll need to clip in the rope to the quickdraw. Normally you'll try to do this when the protection is just above your head and is easily reached without having to stretch up too far. This requires a little dexterity on the part of the leader. Basically you'll use the rope to open the gate of the karabiner and allow the rope to slide in to it.

Learning to clip the rope into runners is an essential skill. Efficient clipping techniques will conserve energy in the long term and increase safety. Many climbers develop their own way of clipping in the rope to runners but any method should use the rope to open the gate of the karabiner. Using one finger to stabilise the karabiner whilst gripping the rope between the forefinger and thumb is one method.

The thumb can push the rope on to the gate of the karabiner and as it touches it should automatically slide into position. This is where curved gate snaplinks really come into their own as the curve acts as a captive scoop for the rope.

Hanging on with one hand, strength waning rapidly, usually makes for a frantic grab and clip! If you fail to make the clip and fall off you have added slack in the system which could significantly increase the length of your fall. An attentive second is essential in this scenario.

As you pull up the rope the belayer will need to anticipate how much you are likely to need to reach the clip – this is a skill that is learnt only through considerable practice so be patient in these early stages. Paying out the rope is a simple matter of pulling it through the device with one hand and pushing it through with the other.

Once you have clipped in to the protection the belayer will need to take in any spare slack that develops until you reach a point where your tie in is level with the protection. After this the belayer will need to pay out the rope.

Repeat this procedure all the way to the top of the climb at each point of protection. When you reach the top you must clip your rope into the lowering off point in exactly the same way as you clipped into the running belays. Once you are clipped in tell your second that you have done so and they can then take the rope tight before commencing the lower back to the ground.

The only thing that might cause you difficulties indoors is that you choose a climb that is a bit too difficult for your first lead and you find that you are having to hang on with

A successful clip of a runner high above your head is always comforting. It gives you the opportunity to climb for a short distance with a rope from above. To make a long stretch to clip runners you normally need to have quite good handholds and footholds. As the leader moves up towards the runner the second will need to take in the rope.

When the runner is level with your tie-in point the second will need to begin paying out the rope again.

tired arms making it very insecure to take a hand off to pull up the rope and clip it in. Save this experience for later on in your climbing career and choose something simple for early leading practice.

Leading a sport climb outdoors presents a few more problems for the leader than the simplistic set up at indoor venues.

Firstly you'll need to carry a sufficient number of quickdraws on your harness to clip all the bolts on a climb. Ten quickdraws is normally enough but twelve is often more comforting. Much depends on the length of the pitch you will climb. Mostly you'll begin on climbs of 25m (82ft) or less but as you progress through the grades you may find that climbs become longer. Nowadays many bolted sport climbs are 35m (115ft) in length and occasionally longer.

As you climb you'll need to clip a quickdraw into each bolt before you can clip the rope in. This is where efficiency of clipping begins to play an important role. The quicker and more smoothly it can be done, the less energy it requires.

When you reach the top of the climb it is not likely that you'll have the luxury of a lower-off karabiner to clip into. What you'll find could be very different – it may be two large open bolts through which you have to thread the rope or two bolts linked together with a chain and a fixed permanently closed karabiner or maillon to thread the rope through.

You'll need to be meticulous in dealing with this for safety's sake.

All you need for a sports climb are sufficient quickdraws, an extra screwgate karabiner and a short sling. Carry the quickdraws on gear loops on your harness and make sure that you have some on either side – you never know which hand you'll need to make the clip with.

Be careful to ensure that you do not inadvertently untie from the rope end before you have clipped back in to it. Once you have threaded the rope you can let your second know that they should take the strain and lower you back to the ground. As you descend, unclip the quickdraws so that nothing is left on the climb. Back safely at the base of the climb you can untie from the end of the rope and pull it back through the lower-off.

If your partner is going to try leading the climb you may decide to leave the quickdraws in for them. Or of course they may decide not to lead the climb but to follow it with the rope above them and you belaying from below. In this latter case you may decide not to remove the quickdraws on the way down and leave them for the second to collect on their way up the climb.

Arriving at the top of a sports climb you will need to lower-off the top anchors back to the ground. Anchors usually take two forms and utilise two bolt anchors. One type is where two bolt anchors are connected by a chain and the lower point is a fixed ring or maillon at a point where equal load will be applied to each anchor. The second type is where two large bolts with eyes are placed close together, one slightly above the other. The first is the simplest to lower-off from and the second only marginally more complex.

Occasionally it is preferable to leave all the quickdraws in place for your second to remove on the way up. Routes that weave around a little and climbs that are slightly overhanging will benefit from quickdraws remaining in place as they will help to provide more protection for the second.

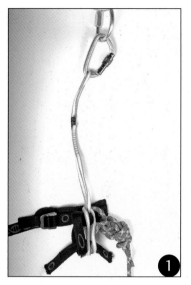

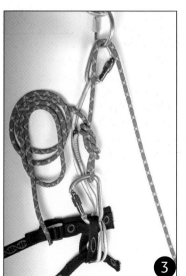

❶ When you arrive at the lower-off, a short sling, looped through the harness tie in loops as shown, can be clipped directly into the anchor. Use a screwgate karabiner for security. If the anchor is a double bolt designed to thread the rope directly through the eye of each simply clip into the higher of the two bolts. Once clipped in you can hang on the sling with all your weight.

❷ Reach down and pull up a bight of rope as shown, thread it through the anchor and then tie a Figure of Eight, not in the bight. This is then clipped to the belay/abseil loop of the harness. **Do not** clip it to the central tie on loop.

❸ You can then untie from the end of the rope and pull the rope through the lower-off as shown. At this point nudge yourself up a little and ask your second to take your weight and hold you there.

❹ Having released the weight from the sling this can be unclipped and removed from your harness if you want to. Shout down that you ready to be lowered and the belayer can begin to lower you down. It's a good idea to practice this technique not too far off the ground before doing it for real at the top of a sports climb. You can rig a practice session by constructing a couple of anchors connected with a sling to one central point (see pages 50–3) and just be a few feet off the ground.

LEADING A TRAD CLIMB

There are many more elements to leading trad climbs where all protection is placed by the leader and all anchors are similarly constructed. It is the most exemplary style of climbing in keeping with the longest established traditions of the sport.

There are two types of trad climbing: single pitch, such as those found on the gritstone outcrops in the UK, and multi-pitch, where the climb is considerably longer than one rope length.

Multi-pitch climbing is more complex and more committing in that it requires the climbers to arrange intermediate stances from where the process of leap-frogging up the cliff can be staged. In single pitch climbing you will arrive at the top of the cliff in a single push.

The key elements to successful trad climbing hinge on the climbers' ability to place sound protection on the lead, to be able to arrange sound and reliable anchors at all stances, and of course to be able to find your way up the cliff face. In all other respects there is little difference to other styles of climbing.

Learning the craft of leader-placed protection takes considerable practice. This experience can only be gained by getting out there and doing it so perhaps it is a sensible suggestion to begin on single pitch climbs or on fairly short two- or three-pitch climbs. Fortunately there is an abundance of such climbs all over the world for aspiring leaders to cut their teeth on.

To begin choose something that is well within your ability as a rock climber. At least if you have little distraction from the technicalities of ascending the rock face you'll be able to concentrate on placing gear during the ascent.

Unlike indoor venues at regular intervals or sport climbs where all protection is in place, in trad climbing the nature of the rock face will dictate where and when you are able to arrange protection. Armed with a selection of different sized nuts and cams the canny climber will be able to arrange protection in seemingly unlikely places. It is vital not to rush the process.

The sequence of climbing the various pitches begins with sorting out ropes and kit at the base of your chosen climb. Time spent being organized at the outset and continuing to do so all the way up the climb will pay dividends in increased efficiency and it is much less likely that problems will arise.

All the protection equipment needs to be carried on the harness so you can expect to feel quite weighed down. Thankfully the modern climber benefits from considerably lighter equipment than even twenty-five years ago!

How you arrange this gear is called racking and how you rack the various tools will be one of personal preference. In the beginning it's good to experiment with different systems until you feel that you have the experience to judge what will be best for you.

Having sorted the gear it's time to set off. Place protection whenever you feel it's needed and if it's available. You probably won't place much in the initial few feet of the ground but try to get something in at around 3m (10ft) or so above the ground. Thereafter take what the rock presents to you – though if there are lots of possibilities you may run out of equipment quite quickly! A sensible distance

between each piece of protection is advisable, say every 2.5–3m (8–10ft) if possible.

If you place a wire runner be sure to extend it with a quickdraw. This helps to reduce leverage on the wire itself which otherwise might get lifted out of its placement all too easily by the drag of the rope.

Having consulted the guidebook description of your climb you'll have some idea of where the first pitch ends. If it's only a single pitch climb it will of course be very obvious where it ends!

A multi-pitch climb showing the different stages or 'pitches' and the stopping places called 'stances' from where you belay each other whether leading or seconding. Climbs such as this – Hope on the Idwal Slabs in North Wales – are ideal early climbs and will present lots of good opportunities to practice rope skills and protection placement essential for trad climbing.

It is vital that you organise your gear well for trad climbing. Pretty much all climbing harnesses have gear loops on either side for clipping all the equipment to. How you 'rack' your gear becomes a very personal matter. The principles of efficient racking hinge around knowing where a particular size of nut or a cam or a quickdraw is normally to be found. You will waste energy fumbling for gear if it is not well racked. Keep nuts of a similar size stacked in groups on one karabiner.

A selection of quickdraws, cams and hexes all racked in some semblance of order. A similar set up can be carried on the other side of the harness. It's always good to have quickdraws on both sides.

Some climbers prefer not to carry too much gear dangling from their harness. It can be quite a heavy load and may feel as though it is dragging your harness off. Here we see an alternative method using a bandolier to carry all the equipment. At the end of the day you must experiment with different systems so that you find something you are comfortable with and stick with it.

Placing a wire-slung nut. Decide on what size you think might fit the crack. Take the bunch of wires of that size and try the one you think might fit in the crack. If you get it first time all well and good! If not you do have other options on the same karabiner.

Once you've decided a particular nut is a good fit make sure it seated well by tugging sharply in the direction it is likely to be loaded, remove the bunch from the placed wire and clip in a quickdraw.

Clip the rope into the quickdraw and away you go! The quickdraw attached to the wire is essential to reduce leverage on the placement as the rope runs through. The last thing you want is for your protection to fall out whilst you are still climbing.

At the top of the first pitch or single-pitch climb you'll need to arrange a stance. This is the position from which you'll anchor yourself to the rock and belay your second as he or she climbs the pitch. Ideally you should be near to the edge of the ledge or top of the climb so that you can look down the pitch to observe your second climbing. It makes it considerably easier to communicate if you can see each other.

Anchors need to be sound and ideally positioned in relation to where you anticipate the load might come from if your second takes a fall or needs some assistance. Normally you try to achieve a straight line in the run of the rope to the climber and the run of the rope to the anchor or, more usually, anchors.

A well-organised stance will make climbing considerably less stressful. Make sure that you are tight to your anchor point and the the line of the attachment to the anchor is identical to the direction in which you anticipate the load might come from if the climber you are safeguarding falls off. The rope that you take in should be neatly stacked on the ledge by your side. Before the leader begins the next pitch of the climb, sort out the gear and run the rope through so that the leader's end is on top of the pile of rope. You may of course wish to share the leading. In this case the Second will arrive at the stance, sort out the equipment on the rack and then head off on the next pitch.

Bear in mind that on multi-pitch climbs this is exactly the same place that your second will be positioned to belay you on the next pitch.

When the second arrives at the top to join you they should tie in to the anchor point in the same way that you have done. (If it's the top of the climb send them off well away from the edge for safety.)

Once the second is secure you can remove the rope from the belay device and begin the process of re-organising the equipment as you were at the start of the climb. It's always a good idea to run the rope through so that the end that is attached to the leader is on top of the pile of rope on the ledge.

The second can now set up your rope in his or her belay device and once that's done you can begin the process all over again. This sequence is repeated until you reach the top of the multi-pitch climb. On most crags you'll descend by walking or scrambling down – very occasionally the descent may require an abseil.

There are plenty of things that you'll learn about multi-pitch climbing as you gain experience. Many will be valuable lessons to store away for future use.

There is much to learn about the ropework skills you'll need for safe rock climbing. Given the basics much of it will be learnt through practical 'hands on' experience.

9 MOVING ON

When you have mastered the basics, had some good experiences and are keen to go further there is an amazing world of rock climbing to be discovered. Beach holidays will be a thing of the past!

MOVING ON

As with many sports, particularly those that have an element of excitement and adventure, it is often a good idea to progress at a moderate pace so that you build up knowledge and expertise without pushing yourself continually to the limit. How long this takes will be different for everybody. A young fit person keen to progress may develop skills very quickly and within a short period of time could conceivably be climbing quite technically difficult climbs, particularly indoors or on sport climbs. If you're older and little bit cronky it could take a bit longer – but persevere. The great thing about climbing is that whatever grade of difficulty you climb at the sense of achievement is the same for all and the rewards immeasurable.

Progression will be more rapid the more frequently you climb. To do this you need to visit an indoor venue or climb outdoors at least a few times a week. This is obviously much more convenient if you live close to an indoor venue or, even better, in the heart of a well-known rock climbing region. It will also help to have few ties or commitments. Those who climb to the highest standards regularly devote their entire life focus to the sport and may climb almost every day. Progress will be extremely quick for folk who can do this. On the other hand you may only be able to get out a couple of times a month to indulge in a bit of rock climbing and to this end should not expect great things to happen too quickly.

There are many more rope skills to be learnt along the way. Many of these skills will be adaptations or variations of the basic themes discussed in this book and some will be entirely different. It will take time and experience to discover the style of climbing that you like best. It may be long easy climbs in the mountains where you carry all your gear with you in a pack on your back and you'll need to learn the rope skills required for moving together over easy but exposed rocky terrain in addition to rock climbing ropework; you may want to climb mountains that require approaches across glaciers, again terrain that requires specific rope skills; or you might decide that big wall climbing where you sleep on the rock face, is where your desires are most easily satisfied.

You may also want to learn how to rescue yourself and your partner from a climb if things go badly wrong. Certainly some basic knowledge of self-rescue is a useful thing for any climber who is committed to the sport.

All these things can wait until you have gained more experience on the rock wherever you choose to climb. For the time being get out and sample the sport, have fun and be safe!

A desert climb near Spitzkop in Namibia.

5 6

7

❶ *A trad climb on Lundy Island. Albion on the Devil's Slide.*

❷ *A sport climb at Cala Luna, Sardinia.*

❸ *Rough granite climbing at Capo Testa, northern Sardinia.*

❹ *Granite climbing at La Pedriza, Spain. El Hueco (The Bone).*

❺ *A classic trad climb in North Wales. Phantom Rib on Clogwyn y Grochan, Llanberis Pass.*

❻ *Desert climbing in Jordan. Supercrack. Climbers on the route show the scale.*

❼ *Possibly one of the best climbs in the world. The amazing Jacob's Ladder on Table Mountain, South Africa.*

GLOSSARY

ABSEIL

to descend on a rope using a friction device attached to harness

ANCHOR

to secure yourself to the rock face in order to belay a leader or a second. You can have single or multiple anchors

BELAYING

the method used to safeguard a climber while he or she is climbing

BELAY DEVICE

the device used to help you safeguard a climber

BELAY/ABSEIL LOOP

the sewn loop on a harness linking the waist belt and leg loops together

BOLT

a pre-placed piece of permanent protection

BOTTOM ROPING

safeguarding a climber from the ground. The rope passes through a pulley style anchor at the top of the climb

BOULDERING

a low level form of climbing and a sport in its own right

CAMMING DEVICE

A device used for a running belay or an anchor in a crack in the rock

CENTRAL LOOP

the loop formed by the rope when you tie it in to the harness as per the manufacturers recommendation

DEAD ROPE

the rope that doesn't go directly to the climber when he or she is being belayed. Sometimes called the 'controlling rope'

FREE CLIMBING

climbing a route using only natural rock holds for hands and feet. Climbers are normally roped together

GEAR LOOP

the loops on a harness where you can clip your equipment to

LEADER

the climber who ascends the route first

LIVE ROPE the rope that goes directly to the climber that you are belaying

LOWER-OFF

1. the fixed point at the top of a sport climb from which you lower back to the ground.
2. To lower a climber off a climb.

NUTS

wedge or hexagonal shaped nuts on wire, rope or tape that are wedged into cracks to make running belays or anchors. Generically called 'rocks' and 'hexes'

PAY OUT

to feed rope out through a belay device. Normally for the leader but a second may ask for slack rope to be paid out

PRUSIK

a knot formed using a thin cord loop wrapped around the main climbing rope. Such knots include the French Prusik used in abseil safety.

PUMPED

tired arms that seem like they may not hold you on to the rock for very much longer

QUICKDRAW

a device consisting of two linked karabiners, used to attach to anchors

REST

to take a break on a climb. Usually a place where you can take one or both hands off the rock.

RUNNING BELAY

protection arranged by the leader using wedge shaped nuts, hexagonal shaped nuts, slings, camming devices or bolts. Often shortened to 'Runner'

SECOND

the climber who follows the leader up the climb

SPORT CLIMBING

a style of climbing where the protection for the leader is in place permanently.

STANCE

a place part way up a climb or at the top where you secure yourselves while belaying each other

TAKING IN

a leader takes in the rope whilst the second climbs up.

TOP ROPING

a style of climbing where the climber is belayed from the top of the climb but walks around to the top to make the anchor and create the stance

TRAD CLIMBING

the purest form of climbing where all protection is placed by the climbers and is removed as they ascend. Derivative of 'traditional climbing'

THUGGY CLIMBING

steep climbing, usually with big holds but it can be very strenuous.

WEB RESOURCES

UK

www.ukclimbing.com
An excellent site mainly for the UK but with lots of news from the climbing world. Superb crag locator with weather forecasts and location maps. Good forum.

www.rockfax.com
Route database. Downloadable topos. Forum. Bouldering and climbing guidebook publishers UK, Spain, Norway and USA pdf of Italy and Greece.

www.thebmc.co.uk
Excellent resource for UK and world news. Access information. Competition climbing. Database. Climbing wall locations.

www.ukbouldering.com
Forum and gallery.

www.climbinfo.co.uk
Foute information. List of guides and instructors. Latest news and new routes. Links to stores.

www.planetfear.com
Lots of interest from the UK and world. Plenty going on and a great resource

USA

www.climbing.com
Great news site. Lots of action and gear reviews.

www.rockclimbing.com
Information from around the world but excellent on USA.

www.supertopo.com
Great photos. Free route guides. Lots of bouldering info.

General

www.thecrag.com
Lots of route information from all over the world.

INDEX